Enjoying Your Bible

Finding Delight in the Word

John Brunt

Enjoying Your Bible

Finding Delight in the Word

John Brunt

OAK & ACORN
PUBLISHING
Westlake Village, California

Enjoying Your Bible © 2020 by John Brunt

For information contact:
Oak and Acorn Publishing
PO Box 5005
Westlake Village, CA   91359-5005

Cover design by Lauren Smith

First Edition: January 2020

10 9 8 7 6 5 4 3 2 1

To the family that surrounds me with love and joy:

My Wife
Ione

Our Children
Laura and James
Larry
Bonnie

Our Grandsons
Marcus
Akian
Conlan

Contents

Preface

Each year I attend an academic, professional meeting of biblical scholars and teachers from all denominations. There are many simultaneous sessions. A few years ago, I sat in on a very technical discussion about the rhetorical structure of Paul's letter to the Galatians. (Doesn't that sound fun?) Three scholars engaged in a vigorous debate. Halfway through the debate, the moderator called a temporary halt for a unique experiment. He suggested that since the first people to experience this letter heard it read to them rather than reading it for themselves (we'll learn more about that in Chapter Two), the debating scholars should hear the letter. At that point, an actor came in and recited the entire letter from memory with significant expression.

When he finished, the moderator called the three scholars back to the table to continue the debate. He said, "We were having a great debate. Let's take up where we left off with this additional data." But there was silence. He tried two more times. Still silence. Finally one of the scholars spoke up: "After such a moving, powerful presentation of this message of God's grace, it seems to me that theological quibbling is inappropriate." Then they did something that never happens in these meetings. They gave personal testimonies about the meaning of the message for their lives.

Could it be that in general Christians spend far too much energy quibbling *about* the Bible and not enough listening *to* the Bible? Our goal in this book is to not only help readers listen to the Bible but also enjoy the experience.

We know the Bible is able to instruct us, guide us, teach us, and show us what to believe and how to live. As we say, it is our rule of faith and practice. Too often, however, we find something less than joyful delight when reading the Bible. Sometimes we're not sure what the Bible is saying or how it could possibly be relevant to the kinds of issues we face. And let's face it: sometimes reading the Bible gets just plain boring.

It is the thesis of this book that reading the Bible can and should be a delight and that the Bible is much more understandable than you might think. Our goal is not to talk about the inspiration of the Bible or to discuss all the theoretical issues of divine revelation—our goal is to help the reader experience the joy of listening to the message of the Bible.

This book is not intended for scholars. It is for the typical believer in the pew and for those who may not have occupied a pew for a while. It is divided into two main parts. The first offers some general discussion about reading the Bible, and the second looks at specific sections of the Bible to offer a few tips for enhancing your reading.

The study guides at the end of each chapter are prepared to be used in connection with this book. For each chapter of the book, there are two kinds of activities and questions. The first type is for individuals and the second is for small group interaction and discussion. If the study guide is used by a group, ideally, each member of the group would begin by reading the chapter in the book itself, then complete the individual activities and reflect on the questions in the study guide. Finally, the members would come together in a small group, do the group activities, and discuss the questions. There is one study guide for each of the 13 chapters in the book.

CHAPTER ONE

Can I Just Read and Let the Spirit Lead?

"I just take the Bible as it reads and do what it says! Plain reading; no interpretation." Although such a statement sounds pious and nice, no one really does this. We all interpret, and we all make decisions about what is binding and relevant for us. And we make all kinds of decisions in life without explicit reference to what the Bible says.

For example, some time ago my daughter went on vacation with us. When she returned to her apartment in rainy Seattle, there was mildew on the walls. If you read Leviticus, you will find elaborate instructions for what to do in such a case. It involves things like calling the priest, killing a bird, sprinkling blood, and the use of cedar wood, hyssop, and scarlet yarn. (See Leviticus 14.) We did none of this. We went to a home improvement store, asked what we should use to get mildew off the walls, sprayed in on, and watched the mildew disappear.

Ah, but you say, "That is the Old Testament. We know many of those laws don't apply today. But we do follow everything in the New Testament." Do we really? In 1 Corinthians 11 Paul is quite specific and clear that women should be veiled when they pray in church, but I have yet to see a church that follows that practice.

Whenever we read, we engage in a process of interpretation. Most of the time we don't think about it because we are so familiar with the material we don't have to. When we open the computer and read the news of the morning, we just read, and, for the most part, understand. It's like driving a car. It becomes habitual, and we do it without thinking. Sometimes, however, we read and there is a piece of news that happens at a place we're not familiar with. Then we might get a map to discover where this place is. Or we may find a word we don't understand and look it up in a dictionary. Then our process of interpretation moves beyond the habitual. The same is true with the Bible. We are always interpreting, and because there is a bigger gap between the Bible and our daily lives than there is between the morning news and our daily lives, our need to look something up is probably more frequent. In a later chapter we will see some of the resources that we can go to for this "looking up," so that we can read more easily and with greater understanding.

A reader might ask, do we really need to interpret since we have the Holy Spirit to interpret for us? There is no question that we always need to pray for the Spirit to guide us whenever we come to the Bible. The Holy Spirit, however, is not in the business of doing our work for us while we let our minds go into neutral. As Paul says in 1 Corinthians 14:15:

"I will pray with the spirit, but I will pray with the mind also;
I will sing praise with the spirit, but I will sing praise with the
mind also."[1]

The same is true for Bible study. We read with the Spirit and with
our mind. The Spirit doesn't interpret for us; rather, it helps us in
three important ways when we read the Bible.

First, the Spirit helps us open our minds and be objective.
Look at what Luke says that Jesus did for His disciples after the
resurrection:

"Then he opened their minds to understand the scriptures"
(Luke 24:45).

They needed to have their minds opened because they came to
Jesus with prejudices and misunderstandings about His mission. We
too always bring a lot to our Bible reading from our own background
and culture. And because we tend to assume our own culture, we are
often blind to what we bring to our reading.

I heard a vivid illustration of this from a New Testament professor who had taught in three different countries and cultures: The
United States, an African country, and Russia. He tried a simple experiment with all three groups of students. He asked them to read the
story of the prodigal son in Luke 15 and then underline within the
passage the primary reason why the prodigal became destitute. In
all three groups, the vast majority of the students within that group
underlined the same sentence. But each group underlined a different
sentence. The American students underlined verse 13:

---

[1] All biblical quotations are from the New Revised Standard Version unless otherwise specified.

"A few days later the younger son gathered all he had and traveled to a distant country, and there he squandered his property in dissolute living."

His African students, on the other hand, underlined verse 16:

"He would gladly have filled himself with the pods that the pigs were eating; and no one gave him anything."

The Russian students were different yet. The majority of them underlined verse 14:

"When he had spent everything, a severe famine took place throughout that country, and he began to be in need."

Here's how the professor explained the differences. Americans come from a very individualistic culture with a strong emphasis on personal responsibility. They see the prodigal as destitute because he blew it and squandered his money. On the other hand, the African culture is much more communal. Within the tribe or clan, you take care of each other no matter what a person might have done. For them the most pressing issue is that no one would help him or give him anything. Finally, the professor perceived the Russian culture as quite fatalistic. Whatever happens, happens. So the real problem is the famine that can't be helped. It is beyond the prodigal's control. Three cultures: three ways of reading the story.

Every time we come to the Bible, we bring our own cultural biases, not to mention personalities and past experiences. We need the Holy Spirit to open our minds. (By the way, a useful way of opening our eyes to what we bring to the Bible is to read in a group with other people who have backgrounds and cultures different from our own.)

A second way the Holy Spirit helps in our Bible reading has to do with our hearts. God's purpose in giving us the Bible is not just to provide information but also to transform our hearts and minds. As Paul says in Romans 12:2:

> "Do not be conformed to this world, but be transformed by the renewing of your minds, so that you may discern what is the will of God—what is good and acceptable and perfect."

When Jesus met Cleopas and his companion on the road to Emmaus and opened the Bible to them, their response was:

> "Were not our hearts burning within us while he was talking to us on the road, while he was opening the scriptures to us?" (Luke 24:32).

Only the Holy Spirit can make our hearts burn and transform our lives. That's another reason we always pray for the Holy Spirit when we approach the Bible.

Third, it is the Holy Spirit who gives us the courage to act on what we find in the Bible. I've heard people say, "You can make the Bible say whatever you want it to say." Yet there is a message that the Bible conveys, and more often than we think the Bible is very clear. In a sermon called "By Invitation of Jesus," the famous Scottish preacher of the middle of the last century, Peter Marshall, said this:

> "There are aspects of the Gospel that are puzzling and diffi-

cult to understand. But our problems are not centered around the things we don't understand, but rather in the things we do understand, the things *we could not possibly misunderstand*"[2]

For example, you can't read through the book of Luke and conclude that he wants us to take the position that the poor are poor because it's their own fault and helping them is useless. God's concern for the poor jumps out at you on almost every page. You can't read Paul's letter to the Galatians and conclude that God values men and masters over women and slaves. There are clear moral mandates in the Bible, but it often takes both wisdom and courage to live them out in everyday life. (We'll explore more about this in Chapter Six.) We need the Spirit to guide us in wisdom and give us courage.

Each one of these three issues (objectivity, transformation, courage) would be reason enough to drive us to pray for the Spirit whenever we open the Bible. The Spirit, however, is never a substitute for the use of our mind and reason. God gave us our minds for a purpose. Let's now explore how, with Spirit and mind, we might enhance the enjoyment of reading the Bible.

[2]Peter Marshall, Mr. Jones, *Meet the Master* (New York: Fleming H. Revell, 1949), p. 128; emphasis added.

For the Individual

1. Do a brief assessment of your own cultural background. What is your primary culture? What sub-cultures are also important to your identity? Can you think of ways your background might affect the way you read the Bible?

2. Make a list of regular decisions and actions that are part of your daily life. How many of these are explicitly based on guidance you receive from the Bible? Are there other ways the Bible guides you that are less specific?

3. When was the last time you felt your heart burning within you after an encounter with the Bible? Describe what elicited this response.

For the Group

1. Have someone read out loud the following parable from Matthew 20:1-16 (NRSV) while the members of the group listen.

   "For the kingdom of heaven is like a landowner who went out early in the morning to hire laborers for his vineyard. After agreeing with the laborers for the usual daily wage, he sent them into his vineyard. When he went out about nine o'clock, he saw others standing idle in the marketplace; and he said to them, 'You also go into the vineyard, and I will pay you whatever is right.' So they went. When he went out again about noon and about three o'clock, he did the same. And about five o'clock he went out and found others standing around; and he said to them, 'Why are you standing here idle all day?' They said to him, 'Because no one has hired us.' He said to them, 'You also go into the vineyard.' When evening came, the owner of the vineyard said to his manager, 'Call the laborers and give them their pay, beginning with the last and then going to the first.' When those hired about five o'clock came, each of them received the usual daily wage. Now when the first came, they thought they would receive more; but each of them also received the usual daily wage. And when they received it, they grumbled against the landowner, saying, 'These last worked only one hour, and you have made them equal to us who have borne the burden of the day and the scorching heat.' But he replied to one of them, 'Friend, I am doing you no wrong; did you not agree with me for the usual daily wage? Take what belongs to you and go; I choose to give to this last the same as I give to you. Am I not allowed to do what I choose with what belongs to me? Or are you envious because I am generous?' So the last will be first, and the first will be last."

2. Have each member of the group privately make a list of the two or three points that Jesus makes in this parable about the kingdom of heaven.

3. Have each member of the group write one sentence expressing their feelings about this parable.

4. Have the group compare and contrast both lists. Then discuss how the points you see and the way you feel about the parable might be related to each person's background, culture, and sub-culture.

5. Of the three roles of the Holy Spirit in Bible study presented in the chapter, which do think is most important and why?

CHAPTER TWO

Reading Wholistically

For many years I taught religion classes in a university. Most of my courses explored various sections of the New Testament. Whenever we began the study of a new book, whether Gospel or letter, I always had the same assignment: Read the whole book through in one sitting. Then do it again with a different translation. The response of the students was always the same: "You want us to read the WHOLE book? All at once!"

I tried to tell them that no book of the New Testament was longer than one of their textbook assignments in their history classes. (I knew their history teachers and had no doubt that this was true.) But somehow reading that big a chunk of the Bible seemed daunting. Many of them had grown up going to church and studying the Bible with lessons that asked a question and then gave the answer in one verse. They were used to reading the Bible one verse at a time. If you find the answer in one verse, why read a whole book?

However, the Bible was never intended to be read a verse at a time. It was centuries before it was even divided up into verses. In fact, most of those who first experienced the Bible didn't READ it at all. They HEARD it. You see, when Paul wrote a letter to a congregation, he had to send it with a messenger. There was no public postal service. The messenger would then read it to the congregation, probably in the weekly worship service. The messenger didn't have the option of stopping along the way and making a few copies so everyone could read it. There was only one way to make a copy, and that was to write it out letter by letter—a long, laborious process. So the people in the church who received Paul's letter didn't get to read it; they heard it all at once.

Now, the eye and the ear process information differently. The eye is more prone to analyze. It can go back and forth. The ear, on the other hand, tends to synthesize. In other words, it tries to grasp the whole. It can't move back and forth. There is no time to analyze the details. The ear has to catch the whole message as it marches past.

And it wasn't only Paul's letters. Most of the Bible was originally experienced aurally due to the difficulty of making copies. In biblical times, writing functioned differently than it does for us. We assume when we write a book that people will read it silently. Biblical authors assumed people would hear it read to them. The purpose of writing was so that it could be "performed" orally.

In this sense, writing in that world was more like musical notation is for us. Few of us would ever sit down beside the fire and read a musical score. Only the very serious musician would be able to read through the score of Beethoven's Fifth Symphony and get much out of the experience. We assume that the musical score is written so that someone with musical ability can make it come alive in sound. In biblical times it was assumed that someone with the ability to read (in most situations, a minority of the population) would make it come alive in sound so the hearers could listen.

What then does that mean for us as we come to the Bible? We probably aren't going to have someone read it to us every day, although I find listening to audio versions of the Bible very helpful. It does mean, however, that we will come much closer to the original intent of the Bible when we read it wholistically, a book at a time, to try and grasp the overall message the author intended to convey.

So let's give it a try and see how it works for you. At this point, stop reading this book (though I hope you will return) and take out your Bible. Open to Paul's letter to the Philippians in the New Testament. Read it through in one sitting in a translation where the language is comfortable for you.[1] You may find some details you don't understand. Questions may occur. Don't worry about that now. We'll talk about how to handle that in the next chapter. For now, just experience the work wholistically—as my students would say: "The whole book, all at once!"

TAKE A TIME OUT AND EITHER READ OR LISTEN TO PHILIPPIANS.

Welcome back! How was the experience? Here are a few questions for reflection on your reading.

Was the letter difficult to understand?

---

[1] Another alternative might be to listen to the letter from an audio Bible. Yet a third possibility (at least at the present time) would be to watch a YouTube video of the present author reciting this letter from memory. That can be found by going to YouTube and searching for June 6, 2015: Pastor John Brunt: "Philippians." The recitation begins after a three-minute introduction by Pastor Alger Keough.

Was there a clear message that spoke to you?

What did you sense about the tone of the letter? How was Paul feeling about the Philippians?

What did the letter say about your relationship with God and receiving salvation?

What did the letter say about sustaining a relationship with God?

What did the letter say about how to live your life on a daily basis?

What did you learn about Paul?

Did you find the letter interesting?

Did anything in the letter surprise you?

Do you have questions about specifics within the letter?

You might want to read through the letter again with these questions in mind. It might be helpful to take some notes. And maybe you would like to go to the book of Acts and read chapter 16, in which Luke tells us about Paul's first visit to Philippi.

Let me share a few passages in Philippians that become clearer to me when I read it as a whole. In chapter 2, verses 6-11, there is a poetic section about Christ and His example. It reads:

"who, though he was in the form of God,
     did not regard equality with God
     as something to be exploited,
but emptied himself,
     taking the form of a slave,
     being born in human likeness.
And being found in human form,
     he humbled himself
     and became obedient to the point of death—
     even death on a cross.

Therefore God also highly exalted him
   and gave him the name
   that is above every name,
so that at the name of Jesus
   every knee should bend,
   in heaven and on earth and under the earth,
and every tongue should confess
   that Jesus Christ is Lord,
   to the glory of God the Father."

Blood has literally been spilled over the theological interpretation of this passage. Theologians and church leaders have argued about what these words mean for the nature of Christ. How did Christ empty himself? What is the difference between human "form" and human "likeness"? What do these terms mean for an understanding of the how the human and divine natures of Christ are related?

A wholistic reading of the letter makes it clear that Paul isn't talking about the theoretical nature of Christ. He is talking about how the Christian believers in Philippi are to treat each other, and he uses the self-sacrificial love of Jesus Christ as an example for them to emulate. That is clear from the context. He doesn't introduce this poetic passage by saying, "Here is how you should understand the relationship between the human and divine nature of Christ." He introduces it by saying:

"Do nothing from selfish ambition or conceit, but in humility regard others as better than yourselves. Let each of you look not to your own interests, but to the interests of others. Let the same mind be in you that was in Christ Jesus" (Philippians 2:3-5).

Paul is talking about the *attitude* that the Philippians should have toward each other. He is concerned about unity in the church, and he doesn't approach that concern by telling them all to agree on their theology—he urges them to relate to each other with the compassionate, caring attitude of Jesus.

Following this passage there is another text that is often misunderstood. In verse 12 Paul tells the Philippians to work out their own salvation with fear and trembling. I have often heard this statement taken by itself, out of context, to support a salvation by works theology. But when read in context, two issues speak against that. First, the context is unity among the believers. He isn't talking about individual salvation but rather the way the believers work out their relationships. Second, his next words are, "for it is God who works in you." Perhaps a better translation would be, "it is God who works among you," since the context is community. This hardly sounds like salvation by works!

Another interesting verse is found in Philippians 3:13 where Paul speaks of "forgetting what lies behind." We usually think this means forgetting past sins, and that is certainly part of it. But in context Paul has just been speaking of his pedigree—all the things that on a human level might give him reason to boast. The list in verses 5-6 is impressive:

"circumcised on the eighth day, a member of the people of Israel, of the tribe of Benjamin, a Hebrew born of Hebrews; as to the law, a Pharisee; as to zeal, a persecutor of the church;

as to righteousness under the law, blameless."

Paul, however, asserts that he now considers all of this impressive resume as garbage compared to the surpassing greatness of knowing Christ. Therefore, in context it is not only past sins that Paul forgets, it is all those things that might commend him to God on a human level and tempt him to boast.

Let's look at one more verse that is perhaps the most quoted, but often misunderstood, verse in Philippians:

"I can do all things through him who strengthens me" (Philippians 4:13).

It is true that, according to Jesus (Matthew 19:26), all things are possible with God. But can I really do all things? If my goal were to be starting center for the Lakers, that would take quite a miracle given my lack of height and my physical abilities. But look at the context of this verse. In the verses that precede this one, Paul has just said that he has learned to face good times as well as times of adversity:

"Not that I am referring to being in need; for I have learned to be content with whatever I have. I know what it is to have little, and I know what it is to have plenty. In any and all circumstances I have learned the secret of being well-fed and of going hungry, of having plenty and of being in need" (Philippians 4:11-12).

Paul isn't saying that everything will always go well with him, nor is he preaching a prosperity gospel that claims Christ will enable you to do anything you want, including being rich and famous (as some preachers deduce from Philippians 4:13). He is affirming that in Christ he can face everything—even adversity, even hunger, even prison.

Are you beginning to see the value of reading the books of the Bible as a whole? Does this example of Philippians start to make the value of wholistic reading clear? And does it make your reading more enjoyable? In the remainder of this book we will try to give hints for how to enjoy various parts of the Bible. In our next chapter we ask what you should do when you read and face questions you don't know how to answer. What are some of the tools that are available to help?

But before we move on, a story. I believe that the kind of wholistic reading we have explored in this chapter is not only enjoyable but has the power to change lives. I've seen it happen. I think of a student in one of my classes. She had grown up in a Christian home. Her father worked in Christian ministry. But during her university years she had somewhat turned away from God and church. She was seriously dating a young man and did not envision churchgoing in her future.

She had to take one more religion class to complete her requirements in this Christian university, however, and the one that fit her schedule was my class on Paul's letters. Years later, when she was a professor at this same university, she gave a talk in a chapel service where she shared what happened when she took that class.

She admitted that she wasn't really interested in the content of the class, but she was interested in getting a good grade. She told the students she didn't remember one single thing I said in the class! (Ouch!) But that's OK. Since she wanted a good grade, she did the assignments—reading each of the letters through twice as we began to study it. And that reading transformed her thinking, her values, and her Christian commitment. She tried to share what she was discovering with her boyfriend, but he wasn't interested. She decided he probably wasn't the right person for her. She concluded her talk by telling the students that God must have a sense of humor. This young woman, who didn't see herself going to church in the future, fell in love with a different young man, whom she married. He is a church organist and choir director, so not only is she in church every week, she is on the front row!

The Bible has the power to transform lives, especially when we read wholistically.

For the Individual

1. Pick a fairly short book of the Bible that you like (no more than 5 to 6 chapters). Read the book through in one sitting without stopping to take notes or ask questions. Just read it through. Now listen to the book without reading along. (If you don't have an audio version of the Bible, you can go to biblegateway.com and find an audio feature.) Take some time to compare and contrast your listening experience with your reading experience. Were they different? If so, in what ways?

2. Spend some time reflecting on your own experience with Bible study. Do you have any kind of regular Bible study experience? If so, has it been satisfying? Have there been barriers to regular study? How do you think you could improve your Bible study experience?

For the Group

1. Repeat the individual experience above by having the group pick a short book. Take turns reading it out loud to the group. When you have finished, discuss the following questions:

   a. What is the overall message of the book?

   b. How does this message intersect with your daily life?

   c. What emotions do you find in yourself after hearing the book?

   d. Are there familiar passages in the book that you understand in a different way after hearing them in context?

   e. Are there ways in which you find the message of the book to be helpful or perhaps even transformative? Do you encounter God through your reading? If so, in what way?

2. Review the story at the end of the chapter. Has anyone in the group ever had a similar experience or known someone who has

had a similar experience? If so, share with the group.

3. See if there are any brave souls who would be willing to share their answers to #2 in the individual experience above. Discuss ideas for individual improvement with the group.

CHAPTER THREE

What if I Have a Question?

Our emphasis in this book is not on detailed Bible research, but on reading—and reading with joy. Yet sometimes when we read, we come across something that puzzles us. Maybe it's a place we've never heard of. Maybe it's a name we don't know. Maybe it's a word that doesn't seem to fit. Maybe it's a practice we don't understand.

Sometimes a bit of background goes a long way toward helping us understand what we read. Sometimes you can't really understand what's going on without at least a minimal awareness of the historical background. That's not only true when reading the Bible. It's true in everyday life.

For example, I have three grandsons. When two of them were still preschoolers (the third wasn't born yet), I bought them each a toy tractor. There was a cabinetmaker in our church, and as a hobby he made beautiful old-fashioned wooden toys. I knew my grandsons would enjoy them. Since my grandsons lived in different cities, both over a thousand miles from our home, I waited to give them their tractors until we took a trip that would include a visit to each of their homes. When I gave the first tractor to grandson number one, he immediately placed it on the floor, tipped it over, and said, "Tractor tipping!" A few days later, when I gave grandson number two an identical tractor, without having any idea that his cousin had received a tractor, he put it on the ground, tipped it over, and said, "Tractor tipping!"

That seems really strange, doesn't it? Why would they both take the same, rather strange action? Actually, it only seems strange if you don't know the background. One piece of information—and it all makes sense. At that time, the movie *Cars* was popular. Not only was the movie popular, every toy store was filled with items from the movie, and my grandsons had most of them. They were both *Cars* fanatics. There is a scene from the movie that involves tractors being tipped over (a takeoff on cow tipping). So when they saw tractors, they both thought of the tractor-tipping scene. What seemed strange makes perfectly good sense when you understand the background.

Sometimes the same is true when we read the Bible. Fortunately, there are resources that can help us when we are reading the Bible and find something puzzling, and the good news is that some of them are free and online. But before we get into the specifics, let's discuss a more general question. Do I really want to be dependent on scholars when I read the Bible? Maybe they will lead me astray. Wouldn't it be better just to read for myself?

Remember what we said in Chapter One about the need for the Holy Spirit. The Spirit guides us but doesn't do what we can do ourselves. The fact is that even though we study for ourselves with the aid of the Spirit, we are indebted to the work of scholars every time we open the Bible. Unless we are fluent in ancient Greek and Hebrew, we depend on scholars who have translated the Bible for us. Some have given their lives for the principle that people should be able to read the Bible in their own language. So as we think about resources to help us as we read, a good place to start is thinking about what version of the Bible we should read.

No translation is ever perfect. There is never 100 percent correspondence between one language and another. Translators always face a choice. Is it better to be literal and try to keep close correspondence between the words of the first language and the words of the second? Or is it better to try and reproduce the idea of the first language, even if it means using words that are quite different? For example, if you were translating a conversation from Spanish to English, and the Spanish speaker responded to being thanked by saying, "de nada," how would you translate? The literal meaning of the words is "of nothing." But that's not what we would say in English. We would say, "You're welcome." The words are completely different, but the idea is the same.

Bible translators always face this dilemma. Sometimes you can't translate the words literally and preserve the meaning. And this goes beyond just differences in words. It also involves differences in culture. I spoke to a translator with a Bible society that translated the Bible into a remote African language. When the readers read Revelation 3:20, they got the wrong idea completely. In that verse Jesus says, "Listen! I am standing at the door, knocking; if you hear my voice and open the door, I will come in to you and eat with you, and you with me." The problem was that in the culture of that tribe, if you went to a person's house and knocked on the door, it meant you were coming as an enemy. If you were coming as a friend, you called through the door. They changed the translation to, "I am standing at the door, calling." In another example, on a remote island in the Pacific, translators struggled with how to translate Jesus' words, "I am the bread of life," in John 6:35. Because no grain was grown on the island, they not only didn't have bread, their language didn't even have a word for bread. They finally decided that since the staple food on the island was sweet potato, they would translate it, "I am the sweet potato of life."

You get the idea. Translation isn't always easy. Hats off to the dedicated scholars who do the difficult work so we can read the Bible in our own language. But how do we decide which translation to use? There are so many. If you want to see just how many there are, and see them all in one place, go to www.biblegateway.com. It is an excellent resource for Bible reading. It is free and contains translations in many languages. At latest count, there are 59 different English translations. So which one should you read?

There is no single answer to that question, but here are some general principles for choosing a translation. First, it should be in language that is most like what you use in everyday life. One of the features of the original Greek in which the New Testament was written was that it was written in the common Greek that was spoken on the street. You will get more out of reading if you are familiar with the style of language.

Second, make sure it is a translation based on the original Hebrew (for the Old Testament) and Greek (for the New Testament). Some translations are simply paraphrases of another English translation. That puts you a step away from the original.

Third, a good translation will include footnotes showing differences in the ancient manuscripts of the original. In the days before the printing press, all copies of the Bible were produced by hand copying. As you can imagine, copyists made mistakes. And sometimes they even made changes because they thought they could improve on the original. It is amazing how few significant differences there are, but a good translation will let you see that for yourself by showing variations in the footnotes.

Fourth, translations that are produced by a committee with checks and balances are generally more accurate than translations made by a single individual. I love some of the individual translations for their creatively beautiful language, but for accuracy I depend on translations that are vetted by a committee of scholars.

The two translations I probably use the most are the New Revised Standard Version[1] (the one used in this book) and the New International Version.[2] But I enjoy a multiplicity of versions. I suggest you read the prefaces of the translations you would like to use, see that they meet your criteria, and then enjoy several of them. Compare and contrast. See which ones do the most to enhance your understanding and your enjoyment of reading.

Even in a good modern translation, however, you will find times in your reading when you need some help. You don't understand a term. A name appears that is unfamiliar. The Bible talks about places that are foreign to you, and you wonder where these places are. Fortunately, we live in an age where we have more resources than ever before for enhancing our understanding and enjoyment of the Bible.

Let's start with the places. It is helpful to have a good Bible atlas in your library. As you read the story of a battle in the Old Testament, you might wonder how far apart the various battlegrounds are. Or

---

[1]Copyright 1989 by the Division of Christian Education of the National Council of Churches of Christ in the United States of America.
[2]Copyright 1973, 1978, 1984 by the International Bible Society.

as you read of Jesus' travels through Samaria, you might not know where that is in relationship to Galilee and Judea. Or you may wonder as you read through Acts where these cities Paul is visiting are located. A Bible atlas will give you maps that cover all the biblical eras. There is an excellent free resource on the internet to help as well. If you go to www.bibleatlas.org you can type in the name of any city and it will not only give you a map showing where it is located, but it will also tell you where this place appears throughout the Bible. You will also find helpful diagrams of important places like the Jerusalem temple that will help you visualize what is happening as you read. Another similar resource is searchingthescripture.net. I also like to use a search engine to see if there are pictures of archaeological excavations of biblical sites as I read.

For names and terms, you should have a good Bible dictionary. Unfortunately, I have not found a good, free online Bible dictionary. There are many that you can buy, however. Check out the preface and see if there is a particular perspective or denominational tie; try to find a dictionary that is objective and based on good historical and archaeological research. Often your reading will be enhanced by knowing some historical background. For example, if you are reading Acts 23 and see how Paul used the differences between the Pharisees and Sadducees to shift the focus of his trial before the Sanhedrin, it would be helpful to read a good dictionary article on Pharisees, Sadducees, and Sanhedrin.

Another helpful resource tool is a concordance. One important way to understand the meaning of a word is to see how it is used in context in other passages. A concordance gives the occurrences of a particular word throughout the Bible. However, often the same word in the original Greek or Hebrew may be translated in different ways within a single version of the Bible. Therefore it is more helpful to see all the occurrences of the original word, no matter how the word appears in English. There is a good, free online resource that enables this. It is called Blue Letter Bible (www.blueletterbible.org). When you go to that site there is a place to search for a biblical passage. Like Bible Gateway, it has many versions from which to choose. This feature only works when you choose the King James Version. Once you look up a passage in the King James Version, go to the tab at the top and click on "Strong's." Then a number will appear by each word, with either a G (for Greek) or H (for Hebrew) before the number. When you click on that number you will see a definition of that word and all the places it occurs in the Bible. I often find when I'm reading Paul, for example, it is helpful to see how often and in what contexts he uses a word when I'm trying to understand what he means.

Finally, Bible commentaries can be a helpful tool, but they can also be a crutch. I try to make sure I read the biblical text for my own understanding first before I move to commentaries. Then I try to focus on commentaries that give helpful historical and archaeological background information, rather than simply focusing on theological opinion. And remember, the goal is reading with both understanding and enjoyment. Don't get too bogged down in the tools and resources and forget what we learned in the last chapter about reading wholistically. On the other hand, the more you know about the background and history of the Bible, the more you will enjoy your wholistic reading.

So in addition to your Bible reading, read widely on the culture and history of biblical times. Read also about the formation and history of the Bible. All this will enhance your Bible reading.

One year I accompanied my wife to a convention she had in Boston. My birthday fell during the convention, and she surprised me by taking me to Symphony Hall for a concert by the Boston Pops Orchestra. The guest conductor for the night was the orchestra's former conductor, John Williams. The program was all music Williams had composed for movies, such as *Star Wars, Schindler's List,* and *ET.* Not only did the orchestra play the music, Williams also explained how he composed for movies. We saw the movie on the screen as the orchestra played, and he showed us how he synchronized the two. That background helped me enjoy his movie scores even more. I hope you will find the same to be true as you use some of these resources and tools to enhance your Bible reading.

For the Individual

1. Pick a favorite chapter in the Bible and read it through in at least four different translations of the Bible. (If you don't have these in your library, you can find many translations at biblegateway.com.) Which translation do you like best, and why?

2. Read Jesus' parable of the Good Samaritan in Luke 10:25-37. Use the resources at your disposal, including those outlined in this chapter, to familiarize yourself with each of the places and groups of people mentioned in the story. Were you able to find the information? Was it helpful for your understanding of the story? If so, how?

For the Group

1. Have each person share their favorite translation with the group and explain why it is the favorite. How much agreement do you find among yourselves?

2. Reflect together on your experience with the Good Samaritan story. What did you find helpful? Share what resources you liked the best and found the most accessible.

3. Use a concordance or the concordance feature in one of the Bible websites to review all the places in the New Testament where Samaritans are mentioned. What kind of picture emerges about who the Samaritans were, how Jesus interacted with them, how that compared with the reactions of others, and how the early church viewed them?

CHAPTER FOUR

Realistic Expectations

I find that Christians with good intentions about reading the Bible often give up because the Bible doesn't meet their expectations. This can be true for any of several reasons. Sometimes it fails to meet the devotional expectations. Readers expect each section of the Bible to read like inspiring devotional literature, but many passages don't seem to fit that bill. Others are dismayed because they find passages of the Bible that seem to contradict other passages. They expect the Bible to be perfect and are dismayed when not everything seems to fit. Still others are disappointed that the Bible doesn't give a more concise and definitive list of doctrines. And then there are those who want to use the Bible to find answers to their everyday ethical and spiritual dilemmas, and when it doesn't they are disappointed. What do we do when the Bible doesn't meet our expectations? Let's look at each of these issues.

First, the Bible is not simply a daily devotional guide. The Bible is extremely diverse (we'll say a lot more about that in Chapter Five). If you just read the Bible through, let's say two chapters at a time, there will be days when what you read is not all that inspiring, at least on the surface. For example, when you come to passages in Leviticus like the following, which focus on laws for ancient Israel, the devotional value may be questionable.

"Then he brought forward the second ram, the ram of ordination. Aaron and his sons laid their hands on the head of the ram, and it was slaughtered. Moses took some of its blood and put it on the lobe of Aaron's right ear and on the thumb of his right hand and on the big toe of his right foot. After Aaron's sons were brought forward, Moses put some of the blood on the lobes of their right ears and on the thumbs of their right hands and on the big toes of their right feet; and Moses dashed the rest of the blood against all sides of the altar. He took the fat—the broad tail, all the fat that was around the entrails, the appendage of the liver, and the two kidneys with their fat—and the right thigh. From the basket of unleavened bread that was before the Lord, he took one cake of unleavened bread, one cake of bread with oil, and one wafer, and placed them on the fat and on the right thigh" (Leviticus 8:22-26).

You probably shouldn't be blamed if this passage doesn't meet the specific spiritual needs you are feeling today. So why read? What should you do? One response might be simply to skip those parts of the Bible that aren't speaking to your devotional needs and focus on those that do. We all probably do that to one extent or another. Yet there is value in seeing the overall message of the Bible. The Bible was not merely written for devotional exercises. On a much broader level, it shows us the whole Judeo-Christian story of God's interaction with humanity, from the creation of the world to the present. Understanding that history helps us understand God. We see how God continues to work with the people in spite of their failure. We see the direction God tries to move people. We see a loving grace that doesn't let people go. All of this comes from catching a glimpse of the whole history of God's relationship with humans, especially those God chose to be agents of grace to the world. Only this wholistic understanding will allow the reader to see the underlying harmony of the Bible. Not all of this great history is devotionally inspiring, but it all helps us understand who God is and what God has done for us. In other words, the purpose of the Bible goes beyond personal devotion.

It can also be disconcerting when the Bible doesn't seem to live up to our standards of perfection. I have talked with many people who are troubled by apparent contradictions in the Bible. As we will see in a later chapter, sometimes the details of an event in one of the four Gospels will seem different from an account of the same event in a different Gospel. There are several ways a reader can handle this. One is to become discouraged and give up on reading. I've seen that happen more than once. Another is to work diligently to try and harmonize the accounts and show that they don't really disagree.

For example, in Mark 10:46 we read that Jesus healed a blind man as He was leaving Jericho, but in Luke 18:35 the man is healed as He was going into Jericho. I have heard some try to harmonize these two by saying there was an old Jericho and a new Jericho, and Jesus was leaving one as He entered the other. In another case, if you read the four Gospel accounts of Peter denying Jesus, and you notice who spoke to Peter in each case, the details seem to differ. I heard one person try to harmonize this by positing a total of six denials.

Neither of these two approaches is helpful. When it comes to harmonizing, we ought to leave it to the musicians. Who are we to tell God how to communicate with us through the Bible? I find many evidences that God is speaking to us through the Bible without imposing our idea of what the Bible has to be upon God. My suggestion is, when you come on such questions, don't become discouraged and don't try to harmonize. Let each passage of the Bible stand on its own and try to understand what God is trying to tell us through this particular writer. When we look at the big picture, many of these supposed contradictions don't seem that significant in light of the Bible's broader message. There is an underlying harmony in the Bible, but it is not always apparent on the surface.

I have heard others express disappointment that the Bible doesn't lay out a more concise and coherent presentation of doctrines. They would like for the Bible to be more like a traditional church creed, with a clearly outlined list of beliefs. I find it a bit strange that we humans would question whether God shared the Word with us in the right way, but I do understand the desire to have beliefs laid out for us. I have seen a number of books that catalog basic doctrines with specific texts after each one. So often, however, these texts are not given with their context, and this may not represent what the biblical author is trying to convey.

Perhaps the manner in which the Bible is laid out should teach us something. Maybe God is more interested in telling us the story of God's interaction with humans than in giving us lists of what we are supposed to believe. This is not to downplay the importance of what we believe. What we believe about God makes a huge difference in how we live. But our beliefs need to be understood in the context of a big picture that centers on God's grace revealed in creation, in the history of Israel, and most decisively in the incarnation, life, ministry, death, and resurrection of Jesus Christ. Doctrines can be dry and lifeless without the story of salvation. There is significant spiritual danger when we overemphasize lists of beliefs without the big picture of God's love, grace, and overall plan of salvation that gives the beliefs meaning. Doctrines should never be ends in themselves. We are not saved by giving assent to certain beliefs but by a commitment of trust to the God of grace revealed in Jesus. I believe the Bible is presented as it is to help us focus on the story of God's salvation rather than on dry, detached doctrines. And when it comes to the kind of personal transformation we talked about in an earlier chapter, we are much more likely to find transformative experiences in stories than in lists of beliefs.

The Bible is more like a great historical epic than a reference book. I have lots of reference books on my shelves. There are general dictionaries, biblical dictionaries, encyclopedias (although I gave up my bookshelf version for one online), foreign language lexicons, grammar handbooks, books of quotations, and tour guides. All of these have one thing in common. I take them down from the bookshelves when I want a specific piece of information. When a specific reference book has given me the information I need, I put it back on the shelf and never take a peek at it again until I need another bit of data it might give me. Too often we expect the Bible to be that kind of reference book: "What should I believe about that? What should I do about this? Let me take the Bible off the shelf and get the answer I need, then put it back until next time."

The Bible, however, was never intended to be that kind of reference book. It is intended to be a continual source for growing in our understanding of God and learning how to live the kind of life that fulfills God's intention for us. It is a narrative—a story—that gives us continual understanding and guidance, drawing us into a trusting commitment to and walk with God.

What we have said here about doctrine is also true of ethical and practical life questions. If you expect the Bible to answer every question you might have when you choose to take a look at it, you will be disappointed. We will say a lot more about this, however, in Chapter Six.

A final area of disappointment for some Bible readers has to do with material in the Bible we just plain don't like and wish wasn't there. What are we to think when God tells people, supposedly the people of God, to go out and slaughter other people? How can we feel good about passages like Psalm 137, where God's people, who have been defeated by Babylon and carried captive to a strange land, express their desire for revenge? Here is what they say in verses 8 and 9:

"O daughter Babylon, you devastator!
  Happy shall they be who pay you back
  what you have done to us!
Happy shall they be who take your little ones
  and dash them against the rock!"

We will explore this question in more detail when we look at tips for reading the Psalms in a later chapter. Suffice it here to say that the Bible shows us the interaction between God and real people. Not all the attitudes you find in the Bible are ideal, because the people in the

Bible aren't idealized saints in stained glass windows—they are real people living in the nitty-gritty messiness of real life. As we will see in more detail in Chapter Six, not everything God commands in the Bible is the ultimate ideal for humans. In the long run, a real Bible with real people in all their messiness may speak to us in ways that an ideal Bible never could. I hope by the time we finish this book it will be clear that the Bible, as it is, is much better than a Bible created out of our expectations would be.

For now, try to put away your own expectations about what the Bible ought to be, and take it as it is. Enjoy both its stories and its Story—the big picture of God's overwhelming love for the world and for each one of us. Pray for the Spirit's guidance and listen for what God might be saying to you.

For the Individual

1. Consider your own experience with reading the Bible. What have been the disappointments and barriers you have faced that discouraged you from regular reading? Are any of them addressed in this chapter? What are others that have not been addressed in this chapter?

2. Are there things that have troubled you as you have read the Bible? If so, what are they? What has helped you overcome the trouble?

3. Make a list of your expectations as you approach reading the Bible.

For the Group

1. Share your considerations from your individual questions with the group. How much similarity and/or difference is there among members of the group?

2. Discuss all the reasons you might give for why God chose to give the Bible primarily as story rather than a more systematic presentation of what we should believe and do.

3. Read the following passage from 2 Timothy 3:14-17 (NRSV) and list the various ways the Bible is to serve the Christian.

"But as for you, continue in what you have learned and firmly believed, knowing from whom you learned it, and how from childhood you have known the sacred writings that are able to instruct you for salvation through faith in Christ Jesus. All scripture is inspired by God and is useful for teaching, for reproof, for correction, and for training in righteousness, so that everyone who belongs to God may be proficient, equipped for every good work."

4. Read the following passages together as a group and discuss the ways that each particular section of the Bible might meet the uses outlined in 2 Timothy 3.

   a. Exodus 20:1-21

   b. Psalm 10

   c. Mark 4:35-40

   d. Revelation 18:1-3

CHAPTER FIVE

Enjoying a Diverse Bible

We think of the Bible as a book, but in reality it is not a book. It is a library. And a diverse library at that. It was written over a period of more than a thousand years by many different people. It also includes many different kinds of writings.

When we read a news magazine, we recognize that not all parts are the same. We read various parts quite differently. We read a straightforward news story hoping that it will give us facts. We read an editorial knowing that it will give us someone's opinion—with which we may or may not agree. Some magazines have a section of poetry. When we read a poem, we aren't necessarily looking for facts but for artistry that speaks to the feelings in our soul at a deeper level. There also might be a section of comedic satire that makes us laugh while at the same time challenging some of our ideas. And we have learned to read all these different sections of the magazine in ways that are appropriate to that specific type of writing.

We need to develop the same sensitivity when we read the Bible. We shouldn't expect the entire Bible to serve the same purpose or be read in the same way. Yet there is a central, decisive focus in the Bible. The beginning of the letter of Hebrews makes this clear:

"Long ago God spoke to our ancestors in many and various ways by the prophets, but in these last days he has spoken to us by a Son, whom he appointed heir of all things, through whom he also created the worlds" (Hebrews 1:1-2).

God has spoken in many and various ways, but God's decisive revelation is in Jesus Christ. God's commitment of loving grace toward humans, ultimately revealed in Jesus Christ, is the central focus of the Bible. Yet as we find in Hebrews, it has come to us in many and various ways. Many of those various ways are similar to the different kinds of writing we might find in a magazine. Part of enjoying the Bible comes when we learn to enjoy the many different genres in which the Bible is written.

Much of the Bible is history. It tells us the story of the interaction between God and world, including both the natural world and the world of humans. In the Bible, however, the history is never simply for the sake of giving facts. It is history with a purpose. Take the Gospels that make up the first part of the New Testament, for example. They give us four accounts of the life of Jesus by four different authors. But none of the Gospel writers wrote simply to give us facts about Jesus. The facts are given to draw us to saving faith. John makes that clear at the end of his Gospel when he says:

> "Now Jesus did many other signs in the presence of his disciples, which are not written in this book. But these are written so that you may come to believe that Jesus is the Messiah, the Son of God, and that through believing you may have life in his name" (John 20:30-31).

Some of the stories in biblical history read like a novel you can't put down. Read, for example, the story of Joseph in Genesis 37-50. It has all the suspense, tensions, surprise twists, and redemptive moments you could ever ask for in a story. Part of the enjoyment of reading the Bible is simply enjoying a great story. As these stories were told orally to God's people through the years, part of the purpose was entertainment. People gathered to listen as we might gather around the TV or go to a movie. Yet at the same time there were always deeper dimensions. Not only are there ethical challenges to the reader but there is also a foreshadowing of how God would fulfill the promise made to Abraham and to all humankind. The sections of biblical history and story always have multiple dimensions.

Much of the Bible is not story or history but poetry. We immediately think of the 150 Psalms, but biblical poetry makes up much more of the Bible than just the Psalms. A reader might not notice this when reading the King James Version, but in most modern translations, where poetry is given in lines rather than block sentences, the reader finds that most of the prophetic writings are poetry as well. Notice the difference between the King James Version and the New Revised Standard Version of Isaiah 45:2-6.

King James Version:

"I will go before thee, and make the crooked places straight: I will break in pieces the gates of brass, and cut in sunder the bars of iron: And I will give thee the treasures of darkness, and hidden riches of secret places, that thou mayest know that I, the Lord, which call thee by thy name, am the God of Israel. For Jacob my servant's sake, and Israel mine elect, I have even called thee by thy name: I have surnamed thee, though thou hast not known me. I am the Lord, and there is none else, there is no God beside me: I girded thee, though thou hast not known me: That they may know from the rising of the sun, and from the west, that there is none beside me. I am the Lord, and there is none else."

New Revised Standard Version:

"I will go before you
    and level the mountains,
I will break in pieces the doors of bronze
    and cut through the bars of iron,
I will give you the treasures of darkness
    and riches hidden in secret places,
so that you may know that it is I, the Lord,
    the God of Israel, who call you by your name.
For the sake of my servant Jacob,
    and Israel my chosen,
I call you by your name,
    I surname you, though you do not know me.

I am the Lord, and there is no other;
  besides me there is no god.
  I arm you, though you do not know me,
so that they may know, from the rising of the sun
  and from the west, that there is no one besides me;
  I am the Lord, and there is no other."

Recognizing that this is poetry makes a difference in the way we read. As we will see in more detail in the second part of this book, when we look at the prophets and Psalms, there are certain common characteristics of Hebrew poetry. One is parallelism. The same thought is often repeated twice in different words or with different poetic imagery. The parallelism can also go the other direction and pair opposite statements. Notice the repetitious parallelism in the passage above. Doors of bronze paired with bars of iron. Treasures of darkness paired with riches hidden in secret places. When we recognize this is poetry, and understand some of the characteristics of Hebrew poetry, it enhances both our understanding of the meaning and our enjoyment of the author's artistry.

One of the common mistakes in reading poetry, whether biblical or modern poetry, is jumping too quickly to reduce poetry to prose and artistry to mere meaning. We want to know what it means, and we quickly reduce this "meaning" to prose. But the author didn't write it as prose for a reason. We lose something not only of the beauty but also of the impact when we reduce poetry to the prose meaning. For example, when God confronted Cain after he had killed his brother Abel, God could have said, "You did a bad thing. This isn't just." What a different impact God's more poetic words convey: "Listen; your brother's blood is crying out to me from the ground!" (Genesis 4:10).

Would you believe that within biblical poetry the genre of comedic satire also finds a place? There are times when readers would certainly have laughed. Of course, as with history, this was not satire simply to be funny and make people laugh; it was meant to make a memorable point. Here is some satire from Isaiah, mocking the practice of idolatry in which the carpenter makes half of the tree into firewood and the other half into a god.

> "The carpenter stretches a line, marks it out with a stylus, fashions it with planes, and marks it with a compass; he makes it in human form, with human beauty, to be set up in a shrine. He cuts down cedars or chooses a holm tree or an oak and lets it grow strong among the trees of the forest. He plants a cedar and the rain nourishes it. Then it can be used as fuel. Part of it he takes and warms himself; he kindles a fire and bakes bread. Then he makes a god and worships it, makes it a carved image and bows down before it. Half of it he burns in the fire; over this half he roasts meat, eats it and is satisfied. He also warms himself and says, 'Ah, I am warm, I can feel the fire!' The rest of it he makes into a god, his idol, bows down to it and worships it; he prays to it and says, 'Save me, for you are my god!'" (Isaiah 44:13-17).

Ah, the comedic irony of worshiping firewood!

The Bible includes other genres in addition to poetry and history. There are proverbs, wisdom literature, letters, and apocalyptic works. We will focus on these in more detail in the second part of this book, where we look at how to enjoy specific sections of the Bible. Notice, however, at this point, that only a small portion of the Bible consists of specific commands or laws, and even less consists of doctrinal statements. Enjoying the Bible means learning to understand and appreciate the different genres of the Bible.

When we think about the diversity of the Bible, we must go beyond differences in kinds of writing. We also need to recognize that there are differences in perspective as well. When we realize that God spoke over a long period of time to different writers with different personalities facing different kinds of situations, this should hardly surprise us. It is more surprising that we find such underlying harmony of the basic message of the Bible. But no one writer can capture the whole picture of God. Nor can one writer convey all God wants us to know. As is often the case in life, truth emerges in the Bible from a variety of perspectives, sometimes seemingly opposite perspectives. Here are a few examples of what I'm talking about.

One perspective we find in the Old Testament suggests that if you do the right thing, follow God, and work hard, life will go well for you. We especially see this perspective in books like Deuteronomy and Proverbs. In the former, God tells the Israelites through Moses that the nation will do well if they follow God but will not if they turn away.

> "See, I have set before you today life and prosperity, death and adversity. If you obey the commandments of the Lord your God that I am commanding you today, by loving the Lord your God, walking in his ways, and observing his commandments, decrees, and ordinances, then you shall live and become numerous, and the Lord your God will bless you in the land that you are entering to possess. But if your heart turns away and you do not hear, but are led astray to bow down to other gods

and serve them, I declare to you today that you shall perish; you shall not live long in the land that you are crossing the Jordan to enter and possess" (Deuteronomy 30:15-18).

The Bible makes similar statements about the individual's personal choices as well. Proverbs advises that being righteous and working hard leads to prosperity and a good life, as we see in the following series of four proverbs.

> "The Lord does not let the righteous go hungry,
>> but he thwarts the craving of the wicked.
> A slack hand causes poverty,
>> but the hand of the diligent makes rich.
> A child who gathers in summer is prudent,
>> but a child who sleeps in harvest brings shame.
> Blessings are on the head of the righteous,
>> but the mouth of the wicked conceals violence" (Proverbs 10:3-6).

Proverbs 21:5 gives the same idea:

> "The plans of the diligent lead surely to abundance,
> but everyone who is hasty comes only to want."

On the other hand, the book of Job demonstrates that a person can be righteous and follow God, and terrible things can still happen. His friends try to convince him that all his woes are the result of some terrible sin he committed, but Job refuses to accept their verdict. Similarly, the psalmist in Psalm 10 can complain that the wicked seem to be the ones who prosper in life.

So which is it? Life teaches us that both perspectives have their truth. It is true that, all things being equal, the one who gets out and works hard will end up with more than the one who lies on the couch and watches TV all day. Proverbs gives good advice for general situations. But all things are not always equal. In a sinful world life has unfair surprises that come to the just and the unjust. We find truth in both perspectives, and a healthy balance when we take both together.

Another difference in perspective comes in the area of Israel's worship and sacrifice. When you read the book of Leviticus, you find detailed instructions on the sacrifices that Israel is to bring to God as part of its worship. Yet the prophets can shout out against sacrifice. Isaiah gives this word from the Lord:

> "What to me is the multitude of your sacrifices?
>   says the Lord;
> I have had enough of burnt offerings of rams
>   and the fat of fed beasts;
> I do not delight in the blood of bulls,
>   or of lambs, or of goats.
> When you come to appear before me,
>   who asked this from your hand?
>   Trample my courts no more;
> bringing offerings is futile;
>   incense is an abomination to me" (Isaiah 1:11-13).

So does God want sacrifices or not? Jesus made it clear that sacrifices are only of value if they lead to a change of heart and action. At least twice He referred to the prophetic criticism of sacrifice without mercy in Hosea 6:6. When He was criticized by the Pharisees for eating with tax collectors and sinners, He said:

"Go and learn what this means, 'I desire mercy, not sacrifice.'
For I have come to call not the righteous but sinners" (Matthew 9:13).

And when He was criticized for letting His disciples pluck grain as they walked through a wheat field on Sabbath, He said:

"But if you had known what this means, 'I desire mercy and not sacrifice,' you would not have condemned the guiltless" (Matthew 12:7).

What we find from the different perspectives within the Bible is balance. Remember what we saw in Chapter One about the need for approaching the Bible with our minds. We use our minds, under the guidance of the Spirit, to find the balance of various perspectives as they apply to our lives. This is why we need to emphasize the underlying harmony of the Bible and find the balance its varying perspectives yield.

Our examples so far have come from the Old Testament, but the same is true in the New Testament. The four Gospels give somewhat different portraits on Jesus' life. At times they emphasize different aspects of Jesus' life. For example, as Jesus faced the cross, Matthew emphasizes the struggle Jesus endured. When He took the three closest disciples into the garden of Gethsemane with Him and asked them to pray, we read:

"Then he said to them, 'I am deeply grieved, even to death; remain here, and stay awake with me.' And going a little farther, he threw himself on the ground and prayed, 'My Father, if it is possible, let this cup pass from me; yet not what I want but what you want'" (Matthew 26:38-39).

John, on the other hand, emphasizes that even though Jesus was troubled, He was resolute in His decision to go to the cross.

"'Now my soul is troubled. And what should I say—"Father, save me from this hour"? No, it is for this reason that I have come to this hour'" (John 12:27).

It should hardly be surprising that different portraits of Jesus might focus on different aspects of His feelings and actions. No one portrait could capture the whole.

Finally, we see different perspectives in the letters of the New Testament. Since they are addressed to different congregations with their own unique problems, the advice to one particular church can take on a different nuance than the counsel to another. In addition, one author can use language in a different way than another. Notice what James says about Abraham and Rahab.

"Was not our ancestor Abraham justified by works when he offered his son Isaac on the altar? You see that faith was active along with his works, and faith was brought to completion by the works. Thus the scripture was fulfilled that says, 'Abraham believed God, and it was reckoned to him as righteousness,' and he was called the friend of God. You see that a person is justified by works and not by faith alone. Likewise, was not Rahab the prostitute also justified by works when she welcomed the messengers and sent them out by another road? For just as the body without the spirit is dead, so faith without works is also dead" (James 2:21-26).

But here is what Paul says about Abraham in Romans:

"For if Abraham was justified by works, he has something to boast about, but not before God. For what does the scripture say? 'Abraham believed God, and it was reckoned to him as righteousness.' Now to one who works, wages are not reckoned as a gift but as something due. But to one who without works trusts him who justifies the ungodly, such faith is reckoned as righteousness" (Romans 4:2-5).

And here is what the book of Hebrews says about Rahab.

"By faith Rahab the prostitute did not perish with those who were disobedient, because she had received the spies in peace" (Hebrews 11:31).

Paul, James, and the book of Hebrews all emphasize the need for faith, as well as the need for faith to be lived out in a life of ethical responsibility. Yet they have different ways of saying it. I suspect that if we put them all together on a panel to discuss these texts, it would be an interesting discussion. There might even be some debate. But I also think they would find that they agreed on the need for both faith and an ethical life. We would probably learn from their different perspectives and come to see a transcending harmony at the foundation of each.

If God chose to give us the Bible with such splendid diversity of time, authors, genres of writing, ways of thinking, and perspectives, I believe our Bible reading will be enhanced when we learn to appreciate this diversity rather than being troubled by it. I also believe that the more we read our wonderfully diverse Bibles, the more we will see how such rich diversity yields a coherent picture of God's gracious love and of our appropriate response.

This also suggests that we should hardly be distressed when we find multiple interpretations of a given biblical passage. As Paul says in 1 Corinthians 13:9-12, we all see only part of the whole in this present world. When different interpreters see various aspects of the whole picture, we have an opportunity to learn from the perspectives of others.

In the next chapter, we will look at how we move from the underlying message of the Bible to guidance for our specific life situations.

For the Individual
1. Read each of the following passages and decide what section of a magazine they might belong in, had they been written for publication today. (Sections might include news, story, poetry, opinion, essays, letters, etc.) Are there some of the passages that would not fit with any contemporary genre or kind of writing?
   a. Philippians 2:6-11
   b. Luke 3:1-3
   c. Galatians 1:6-9
   d. Revelation 5:11-14
   e. Judges 2:1-5
   f. Genesis 1:26-27
   g. Mark 1:40-45
   h. Matthew 13:31-32
2. Why do you think so much of the Bible is in the form of story and poetry, and so little of it is specific doctrinal content? What does this say about the purpose of the Bible? Does this have any implications for God's relationship to us and will for us?

For the Group
1. Compare notes on your answers to question one in the individual questions above. Were your answers similar? If you found significant variation, how do you explain the differences?
2. How many genres or kinds of writings can you think of that are used in the Bible? How many can you think of that are used in contemporary writing? How similar and/or different are your two lists? What accounts for any differences you found?
3. Have each person in the group take a few minutes to think about any differences of perspectives in the Bible that might be found in addition to the ones mentioned in the chapter. Then compare notes. How do you account for these differences?
4. If you are a parent of more than one child, think of advice you have given to your children that might seem to come from a different perspective depending on which child you are addressing and when.

CHAPTER SIX

Enjoying the Bible's Guidance

Some years ago, I was the guest preacher at a church I had never attended before. I arrived early for the Bible study that preceded the worship service and noticed that there were two Bible study classes, one on the main floor of the sanctuary and one in the balcony. I sat down at a place in the balcony where I could listen to both classes. They might have been in the same building, but they seemed to be in different universes.

On the main floor, the class members had various shades of grey hair. The teacher would read a question from the Bible study guide they were using. The questions were all about theoretical, theological issues. Then a member of the class would answer the question by reading a single verse. This was repeated throughout the entire class period. There was not a single word in the whole class that had anything to do with how a person might actually live their lives the next week. But the class was very "biblical."

The class in the balcony was made up of young adults, most of them married couples. Their discussion was very much about "real life." One after another shared the problems they were facing in everyday life. Some of it was almost a little too real, as when a couple shared in some detail the steps their physician was guiding them through in their attempts to have a baby. After sharing, the group prayed for each person. It was quite moving. One notable absence struck me, however. Never in the entire class was there any reference to the Bible.

How do we bring these two things together: the Bible and real everyday life? One can understand why it might be hard. For one thing, the Bible talks about a lot of issues that simply don't concern us in our culture. The longest single discussion of an ethical issue in the New Testament is Paul's counsel to the Corinthians about the question of eating food that has been offered to an idol. You have probably never worried about that when you pushed your cart through the supermarket.

On the other hand, the Bible doesn't talk about some of the issues that do concern us. I was in a seminar once where a young high school student asked if I could give him passages to read that had to do with dating. What was permissible to do on a date? What is the appropriate age for dating? What does the Bible say? I could give him no specific texts. I explained that the Bible doesn't talk about dating because they didn't date during Bible times. One parent of young daughters responded, "That settles it for me. Kids shouldn't date. We should do it just like they did it in the Bible." He changed his tune, however, when I explained that, in most of the cultures of the Bible, marriages were arranged and the daughters were married off by the time they were 12 to 14.

So how do ancient books from a variety of cultures very different from our own help us live our lives today? When we read the Bible, can it be more than an enjoyable exercise in understanding history? Can it become of source of guidance that is relevant to our present day-to-day lives?

Let's try a little experiment. Let's look at Paul's advice to the Corinthians about food offered to idols. It would be so easy to write it off as totally irrelevant. But a closer look might teach us something about how the Bible gives us guidance and becomes relevant for the lives we live today.

In 1 Corinthians 7:1 Paul begins answering questions that the people at Corinth had asked him. He says, "Now concerning the matters about which you wrote." In 8:1 he continues this process when he says, "Now concerning food sacrificed to idols." I'm sure the Corinthians were expecting him to give them the right answer. I can hear them saying, "Is it right or is it wrong? Just give us a straight answer?" But Paul doesn't do that. Instead he takes three chapters to show how they should approach such an issue. We won't do a detailed study of the whole three chapters here, but let's summarize some of the things Paul says about the issue. As background, understand that most of the meat sold in the meat market had a portion of it sacrificed in the pagan temple (often next door). Supposedly this helped pass the power of the gods to those who ate the meat.

First, he tells them there is something more important than knowledge about the right answer. Knowledge can "puff up" a person and make them arrogant. What "builds up" (a favorite term of Paul's to talk about strengthening the Christian community) is love.

He then affirms that an idol is nothing; therefore, sacrificing a portion of the meat to it doesn't make any real difference. Second, he reminds them that not everyone is clear about this. Their previous associations with idolatry make it difficult for them to eat the meat with a clear conscience. Paul admonishes those with "knowledge" to have sensitivity for those who might be hurt by their actions. He sets forth an important principle:

> "But when you thus sin against members of your family, and wound their conscience when it is weak, you sin against Christ" (1 Corinthians 8:12).

In chapter 9 Paul elaborates on this and shows how he has been willing to give up even legitimate rights that he might have for the sake of others. In chapter 10 he uses the example of ancient Israel to show that even though an idol is nothing, it is wrong for Christians to participate in idolatry in the temple. This puts one in contact with demons and tempts one with the sexual immorality that was so often a part of worship in the pagan temple. Finally, in the last part of chapter 10, he arrives at some specific advice. Don't worry about what is sold in the meat market. If an unbeliever invites you to dinner, don't ask if it has been offered to an idol. Just eat. But if they point out that something has been offered to an idol, you might not want to eat it. In that case you would refrain from eating out of sensitivity to them. Finally, he summarizes,

> "So, whether you eat or drink, or whatever you do, do everything for the glory of God. Give no offense to Jews or to Greeks or to the church of God, just as I try to please everyone

in everything I do, not seeking my own advantage, but that of many, so that they may be saved" (1 Corinthians 10:31-33).

What appears on the surface to be irrelevant has a lot of relevance after all, for we all face situations where we have the sorts of questions the Corinthians asked. According to Paul, there are some actions that are simply wrong. They violate our basic commitments to God and go against God's will for us. These include idolatry and adultery. But we also learn from him that living ethically is more than simply knowing what actions are wrong and what actions are right. It involves sensitivity to others. We have to weigh both the motives and the consequences of our actions. How will our actions affect others? Will they "build up"? In light of this, here are several ways that the Bible gives us relevant guidance for real life.

Shaping Character

Earlier we noticed Romans 12:1-2. These verses mark a transition in Romans. This kind of transition appears in almost all of Paul's letters. The first part of the letter focuses on the theology of what God has done for us by grace. Then Paul says, "Therefore." What follows is instruction about our appropriate response to God—in other words, how we are to live in the light of God's grace. The "therefore" in Romans reads,

"I appeal to you therefore, brothers and sisters, by the mercies of God, to present your bodies as a living sacrifice, holy and acceptable to God, which is your spiritual worship. Do not be conformed to this world, but be transformed by the renewing of your minds, so that you may discern what is the will of

God—what is good and acceptable and perfect."

The Bible does so much more than tell us what to do. Its message transforms us by renewing our minds and shaping our characters. God wants our actions to flow from a God-shaped character of love. John shows us this when some Greeks came to the temple to meet Jesus and He knew the time for His crucifixion was nearing. John used a word in Greek that we translate "lift up." It had a double meaning at the time. It could mean to lift up in the sense of exalting, but it was also a technical term for crucifixion. John quotes Jesus words:

"And I, when I am lifted up from the earth, will draw all people to myself" (John 12:32).

As we encounter Jesus in the Bible, we are drawn to Him, and in fellowship with Him, our hearts and minds are transformed. But what shape does this transformation take? Here are some of the ways that the Bible shapes character and transforms lives.

By Envisioning Values

Jesus offers a vision of a new kingdom where God rules and the usual values of this world are turned upside down. Throughout the Gospels we see the contours of this new way of life. Jesus says that this new kingdom is coming in the future, but He calls us to begin living its new way of life in the here and now.

Rather than spelling this out in a systematic way, Jesus tells stories that speak to the heart. He challenges His followers to give up their prejudices against the outcasts and foreigners and recognize all people as their neighbor by telling stories such as the Good Samaritan (Luke 10:25-37). In this story one of the hated Samaritans turns out to be the person Jesus commends for recognizing that a foreigner in need is his neighbor. He challenges us to give up our greed by telling stories about the rich man and Lazarus (Luke 16:19-31) and the foolish rich man (Luke 12:16-21). He challenges us to care for others by telling the story of the sheep and the goats (Matthew 25:31-46). He challenges us to give up the quest for status and power by calling His followers to take up the cross and follow Him in self-sacrificial service. After the disciples argued about who should have top spot in His kingdom, He warned them:

> "So Jesus called them and said to them, 'You know that among the Gentiles those whom they recognize as their rulers lord it over them, and their great ones are tyrants over them. But it is not so among you; but whoever wishes to become great among you must be your servant, and whoever wishes to be first among you must be slave of all. For the Son of Man came not to be served but to serve, and to give his life a ransom for many'" (Mark 10:42-45).

The New Testament never uses the term *values*, but Jesus clearly presents ways of life that are a stunning alternative to the usual values of the Jewish and Greco-Roman society around Him—and to the values of our culture as well. For example, one of the four cardinal Greek virtues was courage (Greek *andreia*), especially courage in battle. Jesus, on the other hand, speaks of peace, love for the enemy, and turning the other cheek (Matthew 5:39).

These are the values that will win in the end and be part of the kingdom that Jesus brings in the future. Jesus expects His followers to be so captivated by this vision that they begin to live this way now in anticipation of the future.

Charting Directions

The Bible's culture was different from ours, and God had to work with people within their culture. Jesus shows that some of the directives in the Bible were something less than God's ideal. For example, Exodus 21:23-25 sets forth a principle of retributive justice. Revenge can only be commensurate with initial injury.

> "If any harm follows, then you shall give life for life, eye for eye, tooth for tooth, hand for hand, foot for foot, burn for burn, wound for wound, stripe for stripe."

Jesus, however, says that this rule isn't sufficient for His followers. He pushes further:

> "'You have heard that it was said, "An eye for an eye and a tooth for a tooth." But I say to you, Do not resist an evildoer. But if anyone strikes you on the right cheek, turn the other also; and if anyone wants to sue you and take your coat, give your cloak as well; and if anyone forces you to go one mile, go also the second mile. Give to everyone who begs from you, and do not refuse anyone who wants to borrow from you'" (Matthew 5:38-42).

Is Jesus going against the Bible? No, He is showing that God was trying to move people in the direction of mercy and love. By limiting retribution to an eye for an eye, God was limiting revenge. But God's ideal went farther. Sometimes it isn't enough simply to do what the Bible says; we need to move in the direction that God is pushing us.

A prime example would be slavery. In the Old Testament we find all kinds of rules that try to make slavery more humane. That doesn't mean, however, that God ever saw slavery as the ideal. Yet even in the culture of the New Testament, slavery was too entrenched for Christians to abolish it. But the New Testament certainly pushes Christians in that direction. Paul tells masters to remember that they have a Master in heaven and to think of how their Master has treated them when they deal with their slaves (Ephesians 6:9). Paul writes a letter to a slave master urging him to accept his runaway slave as a brother—and hinting not too subtly that he should release him (Ephesians 6:9). And Paul can set forth the principle that in Christ all are equal and there should be no difference between master and slave:

"There is no longer Jew or Greek, there is no longer slave or free, there is no longer male and female; for all of you are one in Christ Jesus" (Galatians 3:28).

Therefore when American slave owners defended slavery because it was in the Bible, they may have been technically and literally correct; nevertheless, they missed the point. It was not enough to stand where slave masters stood in the first century, for the Bible was pushing in a direction that would end slavery. To be faithful to the Bible we have to let it continue to move us in the direction of God's ideal.

I know some people become very uncomfortable with this idea. They want to make sure they are taking the Bible literally. But as Paul says, "the letter kills, but the Spirit gives life" (2 Corinthians 3:6). Even today the Bible continues to move us along trajectories that point out the direction we should moving. The equality of all people, including women, is certainly one such issue.

You see, it is possible to be so literal you miss the point. I found that out when I ordered a sandwich at a baseball game. I'm a vegetarian, and at one of the concession stands at Dodger Stadium I could order a burger without the meat. It made a nice sandwich—a hamburger bun with lettuce, pickles, onions, tomatoes, and sauce. Once when I ordered it, the woman at the register called back to the chef that she wanted a burger with no meat: just with lettuce, pickles, onions, tomatoes, and sauce. When I opened the package, I found that he had been very literal. Just lettuce, pickles, onions, tomatoes, and sauce—no bun. It is possible to be overly literal. It can happen with the Bible as well.

By Providing Examples

Moral guidance also comes from the many human examples of faith and lack of faith in the history and stories of the Bible. We see tragic examples of those who let a fatal flaw of character bring their downfall. Samson comes to mind. (See Judges 13-16.) Or perhaps the rich young man who came to Jesus wondering how to be saved. (See Matthew 19:16-22.) We also see heroic examples of those who followed God whatever the consequences. We might think of Daniel. And then there are hundreds of common people who simply performed small acts of faithful obedience that inform us about God's will, such as the poor widow who put her offering in when she thought no one was watching (Luke 21:1-3).

Such real-life examples challenge us at a deeper level than simple rules ever could. We identify with stories and can put ourselves into the picture. These examples shape our perceptions of what it means to be faithful to God.

There are more ways that the Bible provides examples, however, than in the stories. In the second section of this book we will read the poetry of the psalms. Many of the psalms are prayers directed to God. From these we learn something about how to pray. We experience a prayer life that is probably much bolder and more honest than most of our prayers. Examples of how people within the Bible communicated with God can both teach and challenge us.

By Giving Principles

In our little experiment with Paul's advice about food offered to idols, we noticed several broad principles that clearly transcend the specific issue at hand. Even though we don't worry about food offered to idols (although when I was in South Africa I visited with Christians from several countries in the region who still found that a live issue in their culture), we do have our own issues where Paul's advice is relevant. How many times are we confronted with issues where we might be absolutely right in our view, but we need to consider how our actions might affect other people? We too face situations in life where our actions might hurt another person for whom Christ died. The principle that we must consider the effect of our actions on others has many applications.

Likewise, the principle that knowledge without love can lead to arrogance can apply to many situations in our lives. And perhaps the broadest principle of all is that we should do everything that we do to the glory of God. Throughout the Bible, if we listen carefully, we will see principles that give us guidance in our everyday lives.

By Giving Specific Rules

Finally, the Bible does contain specific rules to guide us as well. The Ten Commandments in Exodus 20 come to mind. Notice how Paul makes it clear that idolatry and adultery are wrong when he talks about the issue of food offered to idols. There are three very important characteristics of God's law that we must always keep in mind, however.

First, God's law is never simply arbitrary. It is not like speed laws that can simply be changed by a vote. The city council recently changed the speed limits on a street near our house. Which law was right, the old one or the new one? I guess the right one is the one they voted last. God's laws, however, are consistent with God's character. They are not arbitrary. Since God is God, we assume He could change whatever He wanted to change, but God cannot be inconsistent with His own character. Thus God could hardly decide that from now on murder is OK. As the Creator, God knows how we were meant to live.

Second, as Jesus shows clearly in the Sermon on the Mount, God's law involves more than outward action. It reaches the very depths of the motives of our hearts. For example, it is pretty easy to come home at night, look at the sixth commandment ("You shall not murder"), pat yourself on the back, and say, "I didn't murder anybody today!" But in Matthew Jesus says that this law has to do with our motives, and we violate the commandment by simply being angry at someone. That makes the pat on the back much more difficult.

Third, God's law always follows God's grace. We start the Ten Commandments with the first one about having no other gods in Exodus 20:3. But we don't understand the law unless we begin with verses 1 and 2, which read:

"Then God spoke all these words: I am the Lord your God, who brought you out of the land of Egypt, out of the house of slavery;"

The exodus is the great symbol and actualization of God's saving grace in the Old Testament. Before God commands, God saves. This is why Paul follows the sequence that he does in his letters. First comes the message of God's grace, then a "therefore," then the practical advice on how to live.

When we understand all three of these important elements relating to God's law, it serves as important guidance for us in our faith journey.

We are now ready to transition to the second part of this book, with tips for reading the specific sections.

For the Individual

1. This chapter lists several ways that the Bible shapes the way we actually go about living our daily lives. Which of these do you find most applicable to your own life? Try to think of specific examples of how the Bible has been relevant for you that you might share with the group.

2. Read 1 Corinthians 8 to 10. List as many ways as you can that these three chapters might address actual life in the 21st century.

3. Which section or book of the Bible do you find most helpful to you in making decisions about your daily life?

For the Group

1. Compare notes on your answers to all three of the questions for the individual. Are your perspectives on these questions similar or different? What do you learn from your fellow group members?

2. If you had been in the church mentioned at the beginning of the chapter, which class would you have preferred to attend? How would you have wanted to change the class? How might you have gone about making changes?

3. Read Matthew 5:17-48 together as a group. What does Jesus say about the law? Does Jesus make the law easier or more difficult to keep? What does this passage tell you about the law, what it means to keep it, and how we live our daily lives according to God's will?

4. In preparation for your next group experience, divide the group into four and have one-fourth read Mark, one-fourth Matthew, one-fourth Luke, and one-fourth John. Then come prepared to compare notes.

Introduction to
Part Two

We now move from the general to the specific and offer tips for reading specific genres and sections of the Bible. We begin with the New
Testament and then move to the Old Testament. The four Gospels
will be our starting point, for the story of Jesus is central both to the
Bible and to our lives. However, these chapters are written so that
they don't have to be read sequentially. You can start with any one
of them if you want to begin your focus on that portion of the Bible.

This section is not an introduction to the Bible in the usual
sense. Introductions generally examine questions about the authorship, date, and historical circumstances of each section or book of
the Bible. There are many such books that you can find in any good
religious bibliography, bookstore, or online bookseller.[1] You can also
find introductions to the biblical books in a number of study Bibles
that are available. I highly recommend that you utilize such guides

---

[1]Some years ago, my colleague Doug Clark and I edited a two-volume work that gives this kind of introduction to both Testaments of the Bible as well as to the non-biblical intertestamental literature. Here is
the information: John C. Brunt and Douglas R. Clark, eds., *Introducing the Bible Volume 1: The Old Testament and Intertestamental Literature* and *Introducing the Bible Volume 2: The New Testament* (Lanham,
MD: University Press of America, 1997).

as background to help in your understanding of the Bible. But this kind of typical biblical introduction, as important as it is, is not our purpose here. Nor is it our purpose to be a commentary on the Bible. We aren't going into the details.

Instead, in this second part of the book we focus on practical tips to help you as you read wholistically. These suggestions are more for guiding wholistic reading rather than for detailed biblical research. These tips take several different forms. Some are brief overviews to let you know what to expect as you read. Some are suggestions of literary patterns you might look for. Some are themes that recur through a book that it might be helpful to notice. Some are historical facts that might illuminate your reading or give you some framework in which to set the biblical material. Some are questions that you might want to think about. And I confess at the outset, there is no rhyme or reason to the kinds of tips offered. The suggestions made here are neither carefully organized nor exhaustive. Another Bible student would probably come up with a completely different set of tips. In other words, these are personal, somewhat random suggestions, offered in the hope they will whet your appetite and contribute both to your understanding and enjoyment as you read wholistically. And I have no doubt that your own reading will carry you to discoveries that go far beyond anything that is mentioned here.

So let the adventure of wholistic reading begin.

CHAPTER SEVEN

Tips for Enjoying the Gospels and Acts

When we read the Gospels, we need to develop trifocals, for we always read them with three different levels in mind. The first level is the life and ministry of Jesus. The goal of those who wrote was not simply to convey information about Jesus. They were not dispassionate historical biographers in the contemporary sense. They were evangelists. The very Greek word for *gospel* or *good news* is *euangelion*, from which we get the word *evangelism*. What does this mean? It means that the Gospel writers were writing with a purpose. They were writing so that the reader might encounter Jesus and through that encounter receive salvation and life. Remember what we saw earlier from the pen of John about the purpose of his Gospel.

"Now Jesus did many other signs in the presence of his disciples, which are not written in this book. But these are written
so that you may come to believe that Jesus is the Messiah, the
Son of God, and that through believing you may have life in
his name" (John 20:30-31).

So our first level is the level of Jesus. Why did Jesus do what He
did and say what He said? What was He trying to teach? Why did
His teachings and actions cause controversy? What do we learn about
who Jesus was? How did the various groups in Jesus' day react to Him
and His message? Why? These are all questions we need to ask at the
first level, the level of Jesus.

There is a second level, however. That is the level of the Gospel
writers. They didn't write their Gospels until somewhere between 30
and 60 years after the events of Jesus' life. That's a long time. I'm old
enough to remember 60 years back, and the world has changed a lot
in that time. The Gospel writers would never have dreamed that we
would be reading what they wrote 2,000 years later. They wrote for
a specific audience in their day. In the time of Jesus there were no
Christian congregations. Jesus spoke within the context of Judaism.
The Gospel writers, on the other hand, wrote to Christian congregations. These congregations, like congregations today, had their own
unique characteristics and problems. That is obvious when we read
Paul's letters.

The Gospel writers tried to bring the ministry and message of
Jesus to bear on those to whom they wrote. That, of course, affected
the way they wrote. It influenced what they chose to include from the
ministry of Jesus in their Gospels. John, again, makes it clear that he
couldn't include everything. We have seen what he said at the end of

John 20; here is what he adds at the end of John 21:

> "But there are also many other things that Jesus did; if every one of them were written down, I suppose that the world itself could not contain the books that would be written" (John 21:25).

So why did he choose these particular things to include? Because he believed, under the guidance of the Spirit, that these aspects of the life and ministry of Jesus would meet the needs of those to whom he wrote and lead them to encounter the risen and living Jesus.

The fact that the biblical writers are speaking to their specific time colors not only what they choose to include but the way they write as well. Here is a fairly simple and obvious example. We know that Matthew's Gospel has a more Jewish flavor than does Luke's. Matthew seems to have written, at least in part, to Christians with a Jewish background. Luke's audience probably included Jewish Christians, but he seems to write primarily for a more Gentile audience. This difference affects the way these two writers recount the words of Jesus. (Remember they wrote in Greek, whereas Jesus spoke in Aramaic.) So look at the following words of Jesus as recorded by Matthew in the Sermon on the Mount.

> "'You have heard that it was said, "You shall love your neighbor and hate your enemy." But I say to you, Love your enemies and pray for those who persecute you, so that you may be children of your Father in heaven; for he makes his sun rise on the evil and on the good, and sends rain on the righteous and on the unrighteous. For if you love those who love

you, what reward do you have? Do not even the tax collectors do the same? And if you greet only your brothers and sisters, what more are you doing than others? Do not even the Gentiles do the same?'" (Matthew 5:43-47).

Jesus says their love must be qualitatively different than that of the "Gentiles" and "tax-collectors," both of whom many of God's people in Jesus' day despised. But if a person were talking to Gentiles, don't you think these words might sound a bit insulting? So notice how Luke presents Jesus' words.

"'If you love those who love you, what credit is that to you? For even sinners love those who love them. If you do good to those who do good to you, what credit is that to you? For even sinners do the same. If you lend to those from whom you hope to receive, what credit is that to you? Even sinners lend to sinners, to receive as much again. But love your enemies, do good, and lend, expecting nothing in return. Your reward will be great, and you will be children of the Most High; for he is kind to the ungrateful and the wicked'" (Luke 6:32-35).

Luke speaks not of Gentiles and tax collectors, but of "sinners." Do you see how the audience to whom he speaks might make a difference in the way the Gospel writer records the life and message of Jesus? I think the same difference may influence the verse that comes after the words quoted above in both Matthew and Luke. In Matthew 5:48 Jesus tells His hearers to be "perfect" as God is perfect, but in Luke 6:36 He says to be "merciful" as God is merciful. In a Jewish context the word *perfect* didn't have the same connotation as it did in Greek. Greeks thought of an absolute idea of perfection, whereas Jews thought of perfection in more practical, down-to-earth terms. For Matthew, being perfect simply means having a different kind of love—the kind God has that reaches everyone. The context in Matthew suggests that Jesus is talking about inclusive love, not some absolute standard of sinlessness. Luke makes that even more clear by speaking of being merciful. The meaning is the same, but the connotation is different.

This is why we understand and enjoy the Gospels to the fullest when we read with a view to the time of the writer as well as the time of Jesus.

There is, however, a third level as well. Even though the Gospel writers didn't envision readers 2,000 years down the road, they were writing so that whoever read would encounter Jesus and find in Him eternal life. Therefore, the third level of the trifocal focuses on us and our situation. What do Jesus' deeds and actions mean for me? How do they make a difference in my values and visions? How do I encounter the Jesus of the Gospels in my very different world? I believe that seeing how the writers reapplied the message of Jesus to their world can help us as we attempt to make them come alive for us and our world. Thus, trifocals. So let's begin to try it out and see if it really does help us.

The Gospel of Mark

It is probably best to start your reading of the Gospels with Mark for two reasons. Most scholars agree it was the first to be written, and it is the shortest. Many believe that Mark actually invented a new genre with his work. In the ancient world, we don't find any writings that are the true equivalent of the Gospels. They are not exactly like ancient biographies. A new message necessitated a new form of literature. And the very name *gospel* is significant. It means *good news*, and it was used in secular contexts in the first century world. For example, when a messenger went out and announced that it was the emperor's birthday, that message was called *gospel*.

Here are some things to think about as you read through Mark. First, you will notice there is no Christmas story in Mark. You will also notice there is no Sermon on the Mount or many other things Jesus said that we are familiar with from the other Gospels. Mark is a Gospel of action. Notice how many stories he includes in each chapter and how quickly the action goes from one story to the next. Sentence after sentence often begins with "and," and the word *immediately* recurs frequently. Mark is a Gospel of fast action.

It is helpful to look for patterns in the way the stories are told. For example, stories about Jesus' healing miracles seem to have a set pattern, with the same ingredients in roughly the same order. They begin with a presentation of the problem, placing emphasis on the severity of the case and the inability of others to bring healing. Then there is the action that brings about healing, and finally the response of the onlookers—which is often amazement on the part of the people and anger on the part of the leaders. Another pattern is what is called the "pronouncement story." Here there is some kind of controversy that often results in an accusation against Jesus. The story ends with a statement by Jesus that settles the matter. You can see this in Mark 2:15-17:

"While Jesus was having dinner at Levi's house, many tax collectors and sinners were eating with him and his disciples, for there were many who followed him. When the teachers of the law who were Pharisees saw him eating with the sinners and tax collectors, they asked his disciples: 'Why does he eat with tax collectors and sinners?'

On hearing this, Jesus said to them, 'It is not the healthy who need a doctor, but the sick. I have not come to call the righteous, but sinners'" (NIV).

This is part of a series of five stories in a row, from Mark 2:1 to 3:6, that each end in a pronouncement. It may be that the issues Jesus addresses in these stories were live issues in the church when Mark wrote. And perhaps the occurrence of these patterns is due to the way the stories were told and transmitted orally before they were written down. Patterns help aid the memory of the storyteller.

As you read these stories, try to put yourself in the picture. For example, in chapter 2 when Jesus heals a crippled man whose friends let him down through the roof, look at each of the participants in the story, and then think about your own life. Are there ways in which you are like the crippled man? What are the things that might paralyze you and keep you from being what you would like to be? Are there ways in which you are like the friends, who not only get this man to Jesus but go to some extraordinary means to get him there? Are there ways that you might be like the teachers of the law who criticize Jesus? And finally, have you been called to carry on the work of Jesus in bringing healing to others? Meditate on these characters and make the story more than a historical narrative.

One element that might surprise you is the ending of Mark. In most modern translations of the New Testament, the Gospel ends at Mark 16:8. What follows is usually put in brackets, italics, or a footnote. This is because the oldest manuscripts of Mark do not include

Mark 16:9-20. This seems to be a later addition, added by scribes, largely from the other Gospels, to give Mark a proper ending. It does seem like Mark 16:8 is a strange place to end the story. Some, however, believe that Mark wanted to end the story with the cross as the climax. Whether this is true or not, Mark clearly teaches the resurrection throughout the Gospel. Keep this in mind as you read. See how many places you can find where Mark refers to the resurrection.

There is material in the eighth chapter of Mark that seems to be the watershed of this Gospel. Pay special attention to Mark 8:27-38. Then see how much of this section is repeated again in chapters 9 and 10. What does this suggest about the purpose of Mark's Gospel? How does this show what it means to be a disciple of Jesus? How does the rest of Mark's Gospel flow from this threefold emphasis?

Here are a few other things you might look for as you read Mark. Mark starts out saying that this is the beginning of the good news about Jesus the Messiah. Watch throughout the Gospel to see what this good news is. Also notice how often Mark talks about the kingdom of God. What does Mark tell you about this "kingdom"? There are also some movements to look for in Mark. Notice how Jesus goes back and forth between Jewish and Gentile territory. Do you see differences in what He does in each? Also notice the difference between Jesus' teaching in public and in a house. Pay attention to how many times Jesus tells people not to tell others about what He has done. Can you think of reasons for this? Notice the role of the disciples throughout Mark. How does Mark characterize the disciples' faith? Are they positive or negative examples of faith and understanding?

Look at the role of bread in the center of Mark's Gospel, especially in chapters 6 through 8. How might all of this relate to the breaking of bread in the Lord's Supper of chapter 14? Also try and see if you can find analogies to the story of Israel and the Exodus in the first part of the Gospel. (The "wilderness" might be one example.) What do you think Mark is trying to say about Jesus and ancient Israel?

These are just a few tips for items to be looking for as you read Mark. Now, enjoy reading this first and shortest of the four Gospels.

The Gospel of Matthew

The similarities between Matthew and Mark are obvious to even the casual reader. There is good reason why the Gospels of Matthew, Mark, and Luke are grouped together and called the "synoptic" Gospels, meaning that they are written from the same point of view. As you read Matthew, notice how many of the stories are the same as Mark, often in the same order. Matthew, however, often improves on Mark's language. He leaves out the "ands" with which Mark begins so many sentences, for instance. Since the wording of some of the stories in Mark and Matthew are so close, it seems evident that Matthew actually made use of Mark. As you read, ask yourself why Matthew might have felt it necessary to write a new Gospel that included so much of Mark.

Certainly part of the answer lies in the material Matthew includes that isn't in Mark. Right at the beginning you find Jesus' genealogy. We generally skip over these boring lists of names, but don't move too quickly. Notice how the generations are divided into patterns of 14. What might it suggest about the Matthew's purpose when he emphasizes Abraham and David as Jesus' ancestors? Also be sure to notice something very unusual in this genealogy: the presence of four women. Can you think of reasons why they appear? Do they have anything in common?

In the rest of Matthew 1 and 2 we see the familiar Christmas story that includes the birth of Jesus and the visit of the magi. We often call these magi "kings," but Matthew doesn't do that. There are only two kings in the story, Herod and Jesus. How many ways can you find that Matthew contrasts these two very different kings?

Another major addition to Mark's Gospel of quick action is the presence of much more of Jesus' teachings. There are five major blocks of teaching in Matthew:

5-7: The Sermon on the Mount

10: The sending of the disciples (Mark briefly mentions this)

13: Parables (also in Mark, but Matthew includes more)

18: Teaching on humility

23-25: Woes on the Pharisees and the Second Coming

Each of these blocks of teaching ends with the statement, "When Jesus had finished...." What do you learn about Jesus from His teaching that was missing in Mark?

Matthew also includes appearances of Jesus after the resurrection that are missing in Mark. Why do you think these appearances take place in Galilee?

Here are some other things to look for as you read through Matthew. Do you see evidence of the more Jewish flavor of Matthew? What does Jesus say, for instance, about the law in Matthew? What is Matthew trying to tell us as he repeatedly emphasizes how Jesus fulfills the Old Testament? Matthew usually uses the term *kingdom of heaven* rather than *kingdom of God*. Jews, in order to avoid repeating God's name often used the circumlocution *heaven*.

Do you see any evidence, especially toward the end of Matthew, to suggest some of Matthew's readers might have been discouraged and concerned that Jesus had not yet returned as He promised—or at least was taking longer than they expected? Notice the emphasis on the long time and the delay in the three parables of Matthew 25. What is Matthew's perspective on this question?

A few more questions to think about: Are there characteristics about Jesus that Matthew emphasizes more than Mark? Especially pay attention to the last few verses of Matthew. What do they suggest about discipleship? Finally, when you have finished reading both Mark and Matthew, which one do you enjoy the most? What are some of the reasons for your choice?

The Gospel of Luke and the Book of Acts

First, look at the beginning verses of both these works. It becomes clear that they were written by the same person and were intended to be volumes one and two of a continuous work. Therefore, it is best to read them together. Although we often think of Paul as the one who wrote more of the New Testament than anyone else because he wrote so many letters, Luke and Acts taken together add up to more words than all of Paul's letters. Thus Luke is the largest contributor to the New Testament.

As you read Luke, notice how many of the stories are the same as Mark and Matthew. In addition to these stories, you will also find teachings of Jesus that you found in Matthew but not in Mark, although these teachings are not usually grouped in the same way. Finally, there is also material that is unique to Luke. Try to think about what is new that you didn't hear from Mark or Matthew. How much of this new material do you find? Does it tend to be stories or teachings? Are there particular themes in this unique Lukan material?

Here are some characteristics and themes you might look for as you read through Luke. Notice how Luke, unlike the other Gospel writers, ties the story of Jesus to events in secular history. (See the first part of chapters 2 and 3.) In Luke's telling of the Christmas story, found in the first two chapters, you will find several songs or hymns. What common themes do you find in these songs? Why do you think Luke includes them, when the other Gospel writers do not?

Look for what Luke's Gospel says about the rich and the poor, about wealth and poverty. How many stories do you find on this topic that are unique to Luke? What do you think Luke is trying to say? Also take note of how often Jesus talks about and/or reaches out to people who were considered outcasts in His day (foreigners, tax collectors, women). What do you think Jesus was trying to get across in His day? Do you think the fact that Luke includes so many of these stories may have had something to do with his day as well? And remembering the trifocals we are wearing, how might these stories speak to us? Also keep track of what Luke says about the Holy Spirit, prayer, and the joy of salvation.

When you finish Luke and move to the book of Acts, see if the themes you noticed in Luke reappear in Luke's story of the early church. Pay special attention to the first chapter of Acts. Luke seems to outline the movement of the rest of the book when he quotes Jesus in verses 6-8:

> "Then they gathered around him and asked him, 'Lord, are you at this time going to restore the kingdom to Israel?' He said to them: 'It is not for you to know the times or dates the Father has set by his own authority. But you will receive power when the Holy Spirit comes on you; and you will be my witnesses in Jerusalem, and in all Judea and Samaria, and to the ends of the earth'" (NIV).

Keep a map in hand and try to trace the movement in Acts from Jerusalem to all Judea to the ends of the earth. The book ends with Paul preaching in Rome. How might Rome be considered the end of the earth?

As you move to chapter 2, think about the role the Holy Spirit plays at Pentecost and throughout the book. What is the function of the Holy Spirit in Luke? Why is it such a problem when a man named Simon tries to pay the apostles money for the ability to lay hands on people and have them receive the Holy Spirit?

One interesting feature in Acts is the role of Peter and Paul. In the first part of the book Peter is prominent, but then in chapter 12 he seems to drop off the scene. The only time he appears after that is at the Jerusalem council in chapter 15. In the second part of the book Paul is prominent, but at the end of the book Luke leaves us hanging, with Paul awaiting trial. Can you think of any reasons, tied to the purpose of the book, that Luke might tell the story this way? Is this really a book about Peter and Paul? If not, what is it about?

Here is another feature of Acts that is intriguing. You will notice that most of the time Luke tells the story of Paul's journeys in the third person. But there are some passages where he moves to the second person and uses *we* instead of *they*. As you read the "we" passages, can you find ways that the stories are told differently? (Notice especially the vividness of detail.) How might you explain what you find?

Another interesting feature in Acts is the threefold telling of the story of Paul's Damascus Road experience. Why do you think Luke repeats the same story three times? Are there any significant differences in the three tellings?

Reading Luke and Acts will take some time, but I think you will find the effort both rewarding and enjoyable.

The Gospel of John

When you start reading John's Gospel you will immediately notice how different it is from the other three. Try to see how many differences you can find. Here are just a few to get you started. Notice that John has fewer stories. Instead of several stories per chapter, John often spends a whole chapter on just one story. Also notice how different Jesus' teaching is in John. Instead of the parables we find in the synoptic Gospels, we see more dialogue back and forth with Jesus' detractors. John includes fewer miracles, and he calls them "signs." Notice how many of them have teaching connected with them. For example, Jesus says He is the light of the world and then opens a blind man's eyes. When He raises Lazarus from the dead, He talks about being the resurrection and the life. See how many other instances of the same phenomena you can find as you read through John.

There are a number of themes that appear and reappear throughout John, like the threads of a rich tapestry. Try to track the following themes. See how many places they appear. Then try to think on what John is trying to say with each of these themes. How might each one intersect with your own spiritual journey? Here are some of themes to watch for:

Life

Light

Faith and believing

Water (Notice how often significant events and conversations occur around water or involve water.)

The term "I Am"

The hour

These are just a few themes. I'm sure you will be able to find more. Here are few other things to look for as you read John. Pay special attention to the first chapter. What significance do you see in the way John begins?

Notice the emphasis on the Jews and the notion of being put out of the synagogue. Obviously, John is not speaking against all Jews. In fact, some of his references to "the Jews" seem to refer to Judeans (those living in the southern region of Palestine around Jerusalem) as opposed to the Galileans in the northern part of Palestine. What do you think might have been going on in John's day that causes him to emphasize conflict between Jesus and Jewish religious leaders?

Another interesting theme to notice is John's treatment of John the Baptist. What is John trying to emphasize about John the Baptist? Can you imagine any reasons why John would put so much emphasis on the relationship between the Baptist and Jesus?

Jesus' "hour" is a recurring term in John. There are times when Jesus says His hour has not yet come. Then notice the passage in chapter 12 where Jesus finally says that His hour has come. What is it about this moment that signals His hour?

You will also want to pay attention to the many uses of irony and double meanings in John. Often in John, Jesus' opponents tell the truth without knowing it. Caiaphas, the high priest, makes a statement of pure political expediency. It is better for one man to die than for the whole nation to die. It is a political statement that it is time to get rid of Jesus. But John shows that there is an ironic double meaning to what this calculating high priest had to say:

> "Then the chief priests and the Pharisees called a meeting of the Sanhedrin.

'What are we accomplishing?' they asked. 'Here is this man performing many signs. If we let him go on like this, everyone will believe in him, and then the Romans will come and take away both our temple and our nation.'

"Then one of them, named Caiaphas, who was high priest that year, spoke up, 'You know nothing at all! You do not realize that it is better for you that one man die for the people than that the whole nation perish.'

"He did not say this on his own, but as high priest that year he prophesied that Jesus would die for the Jewish nation, and not only for that nation but also for the scattered children of God, to bring them together and make them one. So from that day on they plotted to take his life" (John 11:47-53, NIV).

John points out an ironic double meaning with profound theological implications in the next chapter as well. The term *lifted up* could mean *exaltation*, but it was also a technical term for crucifixion. Notice how John's double meaning shows how Jesus' crucifixion is also His exaltation:

"'Now is the time for judgment on this world; now the prince of this world will be driven out. And I, when I am lifted up from the earth, will draw all people to myself.' He said this to show the kind of death he was going to die" (John 12:31-33, NIV).

In both these cases John makes the ironic double meaning explicit. See if you can discover other such references that may not be as explicit. The story of the healing of the blind man in John 9 is fertile ground for irony.

From chapter 12 on in John we move toward Jesus' passion. Why do you think John devotes so much of his work to Jesus' passion? Many believe that John 21 is an epilogue, perhaps added later. Do you see any evidence for this view?

Finally, pay attention to the rich encounters Jesus has throughout the Gospel. When you read about Nicodemus, the woman at the well, the lame man, the blind man, Mary, Martha, Lazarus, and the royal official with the sick son, can you place yourself in these encounters? What do these encounters suggest about your encounter with Jesus?

When I have taught courses on the Gospels, I have always had students read through each of the Gospels in one sitting. After they have read all four, I ask them which is their favorite. They always divide themselves over all four Gospels, but not evenly. Although each of the four Gospels is someone's favorite, always more students vote for the Gospel of John. Why do you think this is the case? Which one is your favorite and why?[1]

Now that you have read all four of the Gospels, you might find it both enjoyable and instructive to compare and contrast the way each writer tells the same story in a way that is a bit different. There are a number of Gospel harmonies that place the Gospels side by side to make comparison easier, but you can also copy the passages yourself. Here's a suggestion to get you started. (You might as well start with one of the more difficult passages.) Look at the story of a woman anointing Jesus. Compare and contrast the following four passages.

Matthew 26:6-13

---

[1] For a wonderfully insightful exposition of the signs and themes of John, see Kendra Haloviak Valentine, *Signs to Life: Reading and Responding to John's Gospel* (Victoria, Australia: Signs Publishing Company, 2013).

Mark 14:3-9

Luke 7:36-50

John 12:1-8

What are the similarities and what are the differences, in both content and context? Is this one story, told by four different writers, or is it two (or maybe three) different stories? Do these different passages tell you anything about the individual Gospel writers? What is the main purpose of the author in each case?

If you find this kind of exercise helpful, try it with other passages and see if gives you a new perspective on the Gospel writers as evangelists.[2]

---

[2]For an example of how the Gospel writers might tell the same stories in different ways, you might look at an article I wrote many years ago: John C. Brunt, "A Parable of Jesus as a Clue to Biblical Interpretation," Spectrum, 1982, vol. 13, no. 2, pp. 35-43.

For the Individual

1. Over the course of the week, read the Gospel assigned to you at the last group session. Compare what you find with what was said about that Gospel in Chapter Seven of the book, *Enjoying Your Bible*. What surprises did you find?
2. How would you summarize the message of this Gospel in a paragraph?
3. If you only had this Gospel, would you feel satisfied with your understanding of Jesus? What would you be missing?
4. Is this Gospel your favorite? Why or why not?

For the Group

1. Go back to the exercise in Chapter Seven of the book and compare the following four passages.
   a. Matthew 26:6-13
   b. Mark 14:3-9
   c. Luke 7:36-50
   d. John 12:1-8
2. Discuss the questions asked at the end of the chapter about these passages. To refresh your memory, they are: What are the similarities and what are the differences, in both content and context? Is this one story, told by four different writers, or is it two (or maybe three) different stories? Do these different passages tell you anything about the individual Gospel writers? What is the main purpose of the author in each case?
3. Compare and contrast your one-paragraph summaries of the message of each of the Gospels.
4. Discuss how you were blessed spiritually by reading one of the Gospels through.

5. If the group had to pick a favorite Gospel, which one would it be and why?

CHAPTER EIGHT

Tips for Enjoying New Testament Letters

The Letters of Paul

There are 13 letters in the New Testament that have Paul's name at the beginning. Several of these include the names of some of Paul's companions along with his name. These letters begin with Romans and end with Philemon. They are not in chronological order; they seem to have been arranged during the early history of the church by size, starting with the longest, Romans, and ending with the shortest, Philemon. It is hardly surprising that some find Paul difficult to understand. This seems to have been true as early as the time of the New Testament. Look at what 2 Peter 3:15-16 has to say:

"So also our beloved brother Paul wrote to you according to the wisdom given him, speaking of this as he does in all his letters. There are some things in them hard to understand, which the ignorant and unstable twist to their own destruction, as they do the other scriptures."

Here are a few tips that might make Paul more understandable and make reading his letters more enjoyable. First, remember what we said in Chapter Two. Paul wrote these letters as messages to individual churches with their particular needs and problems. He didn't expect people to pore over them as theological treatises. They were letters. Paul assumed that they would be read to the congregation out loud and the people would listen. Therefore, as you read (or perhaps listen) try to catch the whole message. Put yourself in the shoes of a member in one of those house churches. What kind of reaction might there have been? How might you and your fellow members have been inspired, encouraged, challenged, or rebuked? What would the primary takeaway have been? Try to read each letter in one sitting.

You also might get more out of reading Paul's letters if you understand a few things about letter writing in Paul's day. Scholars have unearthed many secular letters from the New Testament era. There are two major kinds of letters. Philosophers and moralists often wrote their essays in the form of a letter. These are longer letters intended for a general readership and are not specific to an occasion. On the other hand, common people on the street wrote letters for all kinds of purposes, much as we might send an email today. These letters are usually short enough to fit on one page of papyrus, since scribes charged by the page and most people had to rely on a scribe. The letters had to be hand carried by a messenger, for there was no general postal service. Letters include personal letters to members of the family who live some distance away, business letters requesting goods or offering payment, instructions to co-workers, and just about all the kinds of letters you might write today.

These letters took on a certain form, just as letters do today. We often begin by addressing the recipient as "dear" and end with the word *sincerely*. We don't do that in any other form of communication. In Paul's day letters began with the name of the sender, followed by the name of recipient, and then the word *greetings*. After this introduction, the writer would often give thanks to the gods for the recipient, wish them good health, and sometimes give some kind of blessing. Then the body of the letter would follow. The conclusion might send greetings to or from others and wish the recipient well. Here, for example, is a non-Christian letter from the third century in which a girl writes to her mother:

"Isis to Thermouthion her mother very many greetings. I make supplication for you every day before the lord Sarapis and his fellow gods. I wish you to know that I have arrived in Alexandria safe and sound in four days. I send salutations to my sister and the children and Elouath and his wife and Dioscorous and her husband and children and Tamalis and her husband and son and Heron and Ammonarion and her children and Sanpat and her children. And if Aion wishes to join the army, let him come; for everyone is in the army. I pray for the health of all your household."[1]

Paul's letters are different from both the philosophical and moral

[1]A. S. Hunt and C. C. Edgar, translators, *Select Papyri in Three Volumes: 1 Non-Literary Papyri* (Cambridge, MA: Harvard University Press, Loeb Classical Library, 1988), p. 341.

letter-essays and the personal letters. They are more occasion-specific than the former and are longer than the latter. They do, however, follow the pattern of ancient letters. They begin with the name of the sender and recipient. Then where we would expect the word *greetings*, we find instead the words *grace and peace*. Grace, of course, is one of Paul's most important theological concepts, and in Greek it is very close to the word *greetings*. This is followed by a thanksgiving section, which Paul expands. He often uses this section not only to express thanks for the people but also to forecast topics he will take up in the body of the letter. Being aware of this structure can be helpful as you read Paul's letters. For example, you will notice when you read Galatians that there is no thanksgiving section. See if you can figure out why this is so.

Paul usually adds an additional part of the letter that is something like the letter-essays of the moralists but is much more specific to the congregation. At some point in Paul's letters he generally says, "Therefore," and then turns to specific ethical and practical advice for the congregation. Look for this transition as you read, and try to notice the connections between this practical advice and the message in the body of the letter. (See, for example, Romans 12:1 and Ephesians 4:1.)

Since these letters are specific to a congregation and its needs and problems, look at each letter to see if you can find clues about the congregation and its circumstances. For example, in Romans 15 Paul tells us quite a bit about his situation at the time of writing and his reasons for writing. It might be helpful to read this chapter before you read the rest of the letter. In 1 Corinthians Paul mentions a letter the Corinthians have written to him (7:1) and then proceeds throughout the rest of the letter to answer their questions one by one. (Each time you see the term *now concerning* you can assume that Paul is taking up one of their questions.) See what you learn about the congregation from these questions.

Listening with sensitivity to the tone of the letter is another interesting way to gain entrance into the letters. Compare and contrast the tone of Philippians with that of Galatians, for example. How might the first hearers have felt when the letters had been read to them?

There is another feature of first-century letter writing that can be very helpful to understand as you follow the flow of the argument in the body of Paul's letters. When we introduce a new topic, we use subtitles. This chapter begins with one, and another will follow soon. In Paul's day there were no subtitles, but there was a way to signal the beginning of a new topic. There were certain formulas that scholars call "disclosure statements" used to introduce a topic. They begin with a desire for the hearers to know or an expression of emotion, followed by the word *that*. In Paul's writings you find expressions like:

I want you to know that… (Notice this one in the secular letter quoted above.)

I don't want you to be ignorant of the fact that…

I appeal to you that…

I am astonished that…

What follows the word *that* is the topic at hand. Paul doesn't use these a lot, but watch for the places where he does and it will give you clues to what topic will follow.

Probably the first of Paul's letters to have been written was 1 Thessalonians. You might want to begin there. That should whet your appetite for the larger letters like Romans and the Corinthians. There are four letters that should probably be read together, since they all seem to come from Paul's imprisonment and are called the "prison" letters: Ephesians, Philippians, Colossians, and Philemon. Philemon is not only the shortest of the letters, but it is also the most like the typical personal letters of the first century. Notice that even though it is written to individuals, Paul includes the church as well as he writes on behalf of a runaway slave. Although this letter is tiny, it offers much in the way of understanding Paul's ethical stance and concern for "the least of these."

The three "pastoral" letters (1 and 2 Timothy and Titus) sound quite different from Paul's other letters. The language, vocabulary and style are consistent among these three, but they vary from the other letters. See if you can notice this as you read in English. (It is not our purpose here to go into the various proposals for solutions to why this is. You might want to look in a New Testament introduction if you are interested in this question.) 1 Timothy and Titus take a form that sounds similar to a church code of discipline or a ministers' manual. 2 Timothy has features in common with the genre of a last will and testament, familiar from the story of Joseph in the book of Genesis. (See Genesis 48-49.) Some of the common features of this genre are: an expression of previous suffering, an expectation of imminent death, an assertion of continued faithfulness, and instructions to those who will carry on the torch when the writer is gone. As you read 2 Timothy, see how many of these features you can find.

Finally, as you read Paul's letters, keep track of how God's grace remains central no matter what situation or problem Paul is addressing.

The Other New Testament Letters

Hebrews

Hebrews and 1 John are the only letters in the New Testament that don't begin by giving the name or designation of the author. This leads some to question whether Hebrews was actually a letter at all. It seems more like a letter-essay or, as some suggest, a sermon or series of sermons. At the end of the book, however, it does have the features of a letter. Yet even this leaves some ambiguities. For example, when the author sends greetings from "those from Italy," does that mean he is writing from Italy and is sending greetings from the people there, or that he is writing from somewhere else and is sending greetings from displaced people from Italy? Here is how he ends:

> "I appeal to you, brothers and sisters, bear with my word of exhortation, for I have written to you briefly. I want you to know that our brother Timothy has been set free; and if he comes in time, he will be with me when I see you. Greet all your leaders and all the saints. Those from Italy send you greetings. Grace be with all of you" (Hebrews 13:22-25).

The beginning of the book just dives right into the topic, however, in a very un-letter-like way. The fact that no author is named has led to speculation about who wrote it, beginning in the second century and continuing right down to the 21st century. Our concern, however, is not authorship, but some tips for reading the letter as a whole.

Here is the first and most important element to look for as you read this book. Notice how many comparisons are made between Jesus, and the salvation He brings, as opposed to other things people might revere. It would be a good idea to keep a list as you read of all the ways that Jesus and the plan for salvation that He reveals and actualizes is better than what people have known in the past. Ask, "How is Jesus better?" and you will get to the heart of this book. It may be hard to understand in places. The argument can be somewhat technical as it compares what Jesus has done with the Jewish sacrificial system, for example. But don't let the difficulty deter you. The message is clear. This is a book about the superiority of Jesus and the salvation He brings. Keep your eyes fixed on that message. As you read, count the ways Jesus is "better than." And in doing so, grow in your gratitude for the gift of Jesus.

Another element to watch for: notice the back-and-forth between theology and advice about how to live a Christian life. In Paul's letters, we noticed that there is often a transition point where the word *therefore* moves the emphasis from theological to practical advice. Hebrews, on the other hand, moves back and forth. As you read, keep track of how many times you see this movement of transition from the theological to the ethical. In each case, ask yourself how the two kinds of material are related. Do you see a clear connection? What might you learn from this letter about the relationship between what we believe and what we do?

Another movement to watch for in this book is a theme that William Johnsson has written about. He suggests that the book follows the traditional idea of a pilgrimage.[2] See if you can find elements of a religious journey as you move through the book.

Finally, try to follow what the author is saying about the Old Testament sacrificial system. You might even want to go back to the Old Testament book of Leviticus and review some of the elements of that system with its temple, sacrifices, offerings, animals, and priests. Ask yourself whether the author takes a primarily positive or negative view of the system as a whole.

---

[2]William G. Johnsson, *In Absolute Confidence: The Book of Hebrews Speaks to Our Day* (Nashville: Southern Publishing Association, 1979), especially chapter 8.

James

The letter of James has often been compared to the wisdom literature of the Old Testament. Rather than following a sequential argument, such as we see in Romans and Hebrews, James seems to move from one topic to another, and the emphasis is definitely on practical, everyday life issues. Take note especially of what James says about the use and effect of our language and speech, about the need to care for the orphans and widows, about the evils of prejudice, and about the dangers of greed and riches.

And here's another thing to look for in this little letter. Many see echoes of Jesus' sermon on the mount from Matthew 5-7 in this letter. You might even want to review those three chapters in Matthew before reading James and then watch for the echoes as you read through James.

The Letters of John

Even more than in the case of Hebrews, 1 John lacks the typical elements of a letter. It is more like a sermon or essay. Here are some things to look for as you read this short book. What themes do you find that were also present in the Gospel of John? What do you learn about the assurance of salvation? This letter seems to place quite a bit of emphasis on understanding who Jesus is. It is clearly concerned about false understandings. Why do you think John considers these false understandings so dangerous? Also note what John says about the "antichrist." Many are surprised to learn that the term never appears in the book of Revelation. The letters of John offer the only occurrences of the term *antichrist* in the New Testament. What does John tell us about the "antichrist"? Also pay attention to the rich concept of love in this letter.

2 John and 3 John are the letters that in form and length are much like the typical, secular, papyrus letters that have come down to us from the Greco-Roman age. You might want to compare and contrast them with 1 John. Take note also of what they tell us about conflicts in the early church.

The Letters of Peter and Jude

Peter's first letter seems to have a change of tone at chapter 4, verse 12. Up to that point the letter appears to address the possibility of suffering, but in 4:12 the letter focuses on the reality of suffering in the lives of the readers. Many believe that the first three chapters of this letter were part of the early Christian baptismal instruction that welcomed new Christians and gave them both the assurance of their salvation in Christ and instruction on how to live the Christian life. Throughout these chapters keep an eye open to that possibility, and see if you can find any possible connections between these chapters and baptism. The fifth and final chapter of the letter talks about Christian ministry, using the metaphor of a shepherd tending the flock of God under the tutelage of the Chief Shepherd, Jesus Christ. Pay particular attention to the qualities of leadership you find in this chapter. Most of us don't live in a world of sheep and shepherds, but what would this kind of caring ministry look like in today's world? What kind of contemporary metaphors can you think of that would convey the same qualities of Christian ministry?

2 Peter and Jude should be read together. Notice how similar parts of 2 Peter are to the short letter of Jude. (Jude is the shortest letter in the New Testament in terms of the number of Greek words.) You will also want to focus on what 2 Peter says about the second coming of Jesus, and specifically about its apparent delay. What does it suggest

that at this early stage of Christian history there was already concern about the apparent delay of Christ's second coming?

Reading all these letters is a lot like reading someone else's mail, but what a rich spiritual treat it is to see how God's servants met the real-life, practical issues of the early church with the principles and challenges of the gospel and the assurance of the presence of the Risen Christ through the Holy Spirit.

For the Individual

1. Read 1 Thessalonians through in one sitting. This is probably the first of Paul's letters that we have in the New Testament. (Paul's letters are not arranged chronologically in the Bible.) Then consider the following questions.

    a. How would you summarize Paul's purpose in writing this letter?

    b. Do you find any examples of the general, first-century letter writing conventions that were outlined in the chapter?

    c. Do you think there were any specific problems Paul might have been addressing in this letter? Remember you are only seeing one side of the conversation. Can you, however, make any guesses about what was happening on the other side?

    d. How do you read the tone of this letter? Was Paul basically happy or unhappy with the Thessalonians? What specific evidence do you find?

2. Try listening to 1 Thessalonians and see if any of your answers are changed when you hear instead of read.

For the Group

1. Compare notes on your answers to the individual questions. How similar and/or different are your responses?

2. Use a Bible dictionary to learn a little about Thessalonica in the first century. Where was it? What kind of a place was it? Does any of this information inform or enrich your reading of the letter?

3. Discuss what you have learned from your reading of 1 Thessalonians.

4. Has your reading contributed to your devotional life? Has it inspired you? If so, how?

5. After reading this letter, how would you characterize Paul? Is he
   primarily theologian, evangelist, pastor, or what?

CHAPTER NINE

Tips for Enjoying the Book of Revelation

Enjoying Revelation! Really? We don't usually think about enjoying this book. Many people are scared even to take a peek. It is probably considered the most daunting and frightening book in the New Testament. I want to invite you to try an experiment. Without denying the importance of other ways of reading, studying, researching, decoding, and interpreting the book of Revelation, I invite you to read it from a very different perspective than we usually consider. I really believe you will find it useful.

Twice I have had the privilege of sitting in the audience when an actor (a different one on each occasion) recited the book of Revelation from memory from start to finish. The recitation took between an hour and an hour and a half. As we listened to the book in that amount of time, there was no opportunity to try and figure out the meaning of each symbol or compare the various beasts and horns and heads with historical events or entities. We had to simply listen to the whole message. I was surprised at how inspiring, uplifting, and encouraging it was to experience the book that way. It was far different from our usual study of the book of Revelation.

Yet this is precisely the way the people in what is now eastern Turkey, in cities like Ephesus, Thyatira, and Laodicea, who first heard this book at the end of the first century, experienced it. John makes that clear at the beginning. Note how the first three verses get the book started:

"The revelation of Jesus Christ, which God gave him to show his servants what must soon take place; he made it known by sending his angel to his servant John, who testified to the word of God and to the testimony of Jesus Christ, even to all that he saw. Blessed is *the one who reads aloud* the words of the prophecy, and blessed are *those who hear* and who keep what is written in it; for the time is near" (Revelation 1:1-3, emphasis added).

Here are four important things to notice about this introduction:

1. A single messenger read this book aloud. We don't know who this messenger was, but it wasn't John himself. He was in exile on Patmos, an island in the Aegean Sea. A messenger took this work from John and made a circle around the area to the seven churches mentioned in the book and read it to each one, probably in a single worship service. The book was heard, not read.

2. The people in the churches heard this read aloud to them. They didn't even have a copy to follow along. It was through the ear that they experienced the message. No chance to skip around from here to there. No chance to pore over each symbol. They experienced a single, wholistic message. And these were real people at the end of the first century. I can imagine that there was tremendous anticipation as they looked forward to hearing a message from their revered leader who was now imprisoned in exile. I cannot imagine that, after the worship service when they heard the letter read, they went away scratching their heads saying, "What in the world is this all about? John must have gone crazy out there! This letter makes no sense at all." Certainly, John intended for them to make sense out of the message, as is clear from the third important point this introduction makes.

3. John expects the original hearers to "keep" what is written in the book. To keep something must mean to live according to it. John expects this message to make a difference in the way they live. His blessing is not for those who understand the book, or for those who decode the book, or for those who figure it out, but for those who "keep" it.

4. Finally, John's introduction puts Jesus Christ at the center. The message is both from Him and about Him. The central focus is not history (as important as that might be), but Jesus.

So here is the experiment. I'd like for you to read Revelation, preferably in one sitting. Or even better, listen to it read orally. There are numerous ways to do that on the internet. As you read or listen, try to put yourself back in the first century. Imagine that you have heard John tell the story of Jesus and the salvation He brings. You have responded and have joined with a group of fellow disciples of Christ. You meet together in a home every Sabbath. Your faith has been challenged by the difficulty that commitment to Christ has brought. It has sent your beloved teacher, John, to an island prison where exiles do hard labor in rock quarries. In one of your sister churches, the church at Pergamum, a man named Antipas has been martyred for his faith. And now you have gotten the great news that this Sabbath a messenger from John is going to read a message John has sent to us from exile. You are excited.

With your mind back in the framework of that world, experience the message of this book and ask how you would have understood it. What about this message would have encouraged you? What would the most important take-away have been? Would you have found an encounter with Jesus in this message?

Now step out of that world back into the 21ˢᵗ century. Are there ways that this message would speak to your present world? What would it mean for you to "keep" the word of this book? What kinds of challenges does it present to the prevailing culture of your day? Is there a central, enduring message that you find in John's ancient words?

I am suggesting neither that this is the only way to think about the message of Revelation nor that in-depth study of the book from other perspectives, such as a historical one, is wrong. Nor do I believe that the message of the book was exhausted in the first century. We must never forget, however, that when John got to the end of the book he specifically commanded that the message *not* be sealed up for future reference:

> "I, John, am the one who heard and saw these things. And when I heard and saw them, I fell down to worship at the feet of the angel who showed them to me; but he said to me, 'You

must not do that! I am a fellow servant with you and your comrades the prophets, and with those who keep the words of this book. Worship God!' And he said to me, 'Do not seal up the words of the prophecy of this book, for the time is near'" (Revelation 22:8-10).

How did you find this experiment? Was it helpful to you? Do you have a different feeling about Revelation after experiencing it from this perspective? With this perspective in mind, now go back to the book and take a more leisurely stroll through it. Here are some specifics things to look for as you do.

First, focus on what the book says about the Lamb. John uses the term 28 times in 22 chapters. What are the characteristics of the Lamb? What does it mean for the Lamb to be at the center of God's throne (7:17)? How can a Lamb be a shepherd (7:17)? Is this just a mixed metaphor, or is it a profound theological paradox? See if Revelation doesn't draw you into an encounter with Christ when you focus on the Lamb.

Notice the numbers in Revelation—the repetitions of sevens and twelves, for example. Why do you think there are so many sevens in the book?

Pay attention to symbols that are clearly interpreted by John, without worrying all that much about those that may not be as clear. For example, in Revelation 12, John doesn't leave any doubt about who the dragon is. And when you come to other entities that may not be as clear, don't worry so much about what that entity might represent historically, but concentrate more on what it does. What are the principles that drive its actions? How do those compare and contrast with the actions and principles of the Lamb? For example, when you come to the fall of Babylon in chapter 18, ask what is so bad about Babylon. What principles motivate Babylon? Why do kings and merchants mourn her loss? There are significant contrasts in Revelation. The Lamb versus the beast. Babylon versus the remade Jerusalem. These contrasts are not only about entities at a particular time, they are about different ways of life in all times. Maybe if we spent less time trying to figure out who the bad guys are in Revelation, and more thinking about our own lives in terms of these contrasts, we would find out what it really means to "keep" the words of this book.

There is a part of Revelation that is often neglected but deserves special attention. Throughout Revelation there is a whole lot of singing. The four living beings sing, the twenty-four elders sing, the angels sing, the one hundred and forty-four thousand sing, those who are victorious from this world sing, thousands sing, and ten thousand times ten thousand sing. Why all this singing? We are usually so concerned about the beasts, heads, and horns that we pass over the singing, but I believe we get clues to John's theological message when we focus on these hymns. They say a lot about the character of God and of the Lamb, about the assurance of God's victory over evil and death, and about what it means to worship God, yet they tend to be the neglected part of Revelation.[1] See if you aren't blessed by focusing on these hymns. Maybe you will find your heart singing with Revelation instead of being scared by it!

Finally, the book of Revelation has often gotten bad press because it has been interpreted in a very speculative way. I have heard many predictions about the future, supposedly made on the basis of a correct interpretation of Revelation. But they have simply not

---

[1]There is an excellent book, based on a dissertation at the Graduate Theological Union, that focuses on these often-neglected hymns: Kendra Haloviak Valentine, *Worlds at War, Nations in Song: Dialogic Imagination and Moral Vision in the Hymns of the Book of Revelation* (Eugene, OR: Wipf and Stock, 2015).

come true. Many years ago, I heard that Laos, Cambodia, and Vietnam were the kings of the east in Revelation 16, and therefore the Vietnam War would result in Armageddon and Christ would return before that war was over. I have heard presentations that lined up the heads and horns of Revelation 17 with present day kings and popes and predicted that Christ would come by a certain time, but that time has now passed. All this detracts from the true message of Revelation, and it is probably one of the reasons we too often approach the book with misgiving.

So what about those original hearers? How would they have responded? I'm quite sure they wouldn't have left scratching their heads. I think they would have been encouraged that even in the tough times they were going through, when evil seemed to be winning, God was still in control, and in the end the Lamb would win. And I think they would have sung their praises to the Lamb with even more vigor and confidence. Worthy is the Lamb who was slain!

For the Individual

1. Either read the book of Revelation through in one sitting or listen to it in one sitting.

    a. What is the primary feeling that you take away from your reading or listening?

    b. Try to summarize the message of this book in a short paragraph.

2. Now go back and focus on the following passages, all of which include hymns.

    Revelation 4:1-5:14

    Revelation 7:9-17

    Revelation 11:15-19

    Revelation 12:10-12

    Revelation 15:1-4

    Revelation 19:1-10

    Revelation 21:1-5

    a. What are the primary themes you find in these hymns?

    b. What do the hymns say about God the Father and about Jesus?

    c. What do they say about salvation, both now and in the future?

For the Group

1. Compare and contrast your responses to the questions for the individual. Are there common elements in your summary paragraphs? How much disparity is there in your feelings after the initial reading?

2. To what extent do you agree with the position in the book that Revelation would have been understandable to its first-century readers?

3. Martin Luther disparaged the book of Revelation because he said Christ was neither known or taught in it. If you could dialogue with Martin Luther, what would say to him?

CHAPTER TEN

Tips for Enjoying the Torah

The Hebrew word *torah* is usually translated by the English word *law*, but this is misleading. The Hebrew word is much richer than that. It has to do with instruction or guidance pointing the way to how one should live. In the Hebrew Bible, which Christians have come to call the "Old Testament," the first five books are called *torah*.

Before we look at these five books, however, we should say a word about the division of the Hebrew Bible. The ordering of the books and the division into sections in the Hebrew Bible are quite different from the way the books of the Old Testament appear in our English Bibles. The Hebrew Bible is divided into three sections: *torah*, prophets, and writings. Because the largest book in the section called the "writings" was the Psalms, the sections were sometimes called the

Law of Moses, the prophets, and the Psalms. We find this expression in the New Testament when Jesus addressed the disciples after the resurrection.

> "Then he said to them, 'These are my words that I spoke to you while I was still with you—that everything written about me in the law of Moses, the prophets, and the psalms must be fulfilled'" (Luke 24:44).

The law of Moses or *torah* consisted of the first five books, Genesis through Deuteronomy. The section called the "prophets" included much more than we would usually consider as prophets. We would include the major prophets—Isaiah, Jeremiah, and Ezekiel—along with the 12 books we call the minor prophets. But in the Hebrew Bible this section includes books that we would generally label as historical books, namely Joshua, Judges, 1 and 2 Samuel, and 1 and 2 Kings. These books were known as the "former" prophets. Finally, the "writings" included what we think of as poetic and wisdom books, such as Psalms, Proverbs, Song of Solomon, and Ecclesiastes. But in this section were also Lamentations, Ruth, Esther, Job, Ezra, Nehemiah, 1 and 2 Chronicles, and even the apocalyptic book of Daniel. The chapters of this present volume will generally follow the order of the Hebrew Bible, with some exceptions.

Unfortunately, many Christians have dismissed the Old Testament as at worst obsolete or at best an optional prelude to the New Testament. But it is impossible to read and understand the New Testament without an understanding of the Old. They stand together as God's Word. Virtually every page of the New Testament includes quotes from or allusions to the Old Testament. The three Old Testament books most quoted in the New Testament, in order of frequency, are the Psalms, Isaiah, and Exodus. So we begin with tips for enjoying the first section of the Old Testament: the *torah*, the law of Moses, or, as it has been called since the early Christian era, the Pentateuch.

One thing to look for as you read the Old Testament is a seemingly small but important difference in the presentation of one word. The word is *lord*, but when it refers to God you will see it in one of two ways. Sometimes it will have only the first letter capitalized (Lord) and at other times the whole word will be capitalized (LORD). The former represents a translation of the very common word for a lord or master, which can be used for human masters or for God. The latter, however, represents a translation of the personal name for Israel's God in the Old Testament, *Yahweh*. Since this personal name was considered so sacred that it was not pronounced, and Jews used the common word *lord* instead, most versions use the all caps LORD to refer to Yahweh.

There is much debate about the origin, history, and transmission of the Pentateuch. Although traditionally called the five books of Moses, even a cursory reading shows that all five books were not simply penned by Moses himself. For example, Deuteronomy recounts his death. You might want to familiarize yourself with the issues of authorship and sources, but those questions are beyond the scope of this work, which focuses on tips for making your reading more enjoyable. It might be interesting for you, however, to look for evidence of editing and the use of sources as you read.

Here is the most important element to look for as you read through these five books. Take note of a recurring pattern. You will find it over and over again, and it starts right at the beginning of Genesis. The movement goes from divine faithfulness, to human failure, back to divine faithfulness. See how many times you see this pattern of God's faithfulness in spite of human failure, and God's unwillingness to give up on humans, and especially Israel, the people of God.

The first 11 chapters of Genesis tell the story of beginnings, answering the questions about who humans are and why we are here. Try to ask yourself what these chapters on the beginnings tell you about human life, about the presence of evil in the world, and about why we are here. Also ask what they tell you about God. Compare and contrast the two accounts of creation in the first two chapters of Genesis, not looking for little details but for the big picture of God and His relationship to the world. When I read these two chapters I can't help but think of the words of a hymn that refers to God by singing: "Center and soul of every sphere, yet to each loving heart how near!"[1] Which of the two chapters pictures the God who is the center and soul of every sphere, and which shows the nearness of God? See if this difference in perspective also carries over into what is said about the origin and purpose of marriage in the two chapters. You also might find it useful to read some of the other creation stories from ancient times, such as the *enuma elish*.[2] How is the Genesis creation different from these? How is the moral character of Yahweh different from the gods portrayed in these stories?

From chapter 12 on, the scene moves to God's choice of a people who will be faithful to Yahweh and will reveal His gracious rule to the world. God calls Abraham to be the father of the nation that will become His witness to the world. From the very beginning it is clear that Yahweh cares not only for Israel, for Abraham is to be the father of many nations and is to bless all nations. When God first calls Abra-

[1] "Lord of All Being, Throned Afar" by Oliver Wendell Holmes, 1848.
[2] The full text is available online from several sources.

ham we read:

> "Now the Lord said to Abram, 'Go from your country and your kindred and your father's house to the land that I will show you. I will make of you a great nation, and I will bless you, and make your name great, so that you will be a blessing. I will bless those who bless you, and the one who curses you I will curse; and in you all the families of the earth shall be blessed'" (Genesis 12:1-3).

And before God brought judgment on Sodom and Gomorrah, He asked:

> "The Lord said, 'Shall I hide from Abraham what I am about to do, seeing that Abraham shall become a great and mighty nation, and all the nations of the earth shall be blessed in him?'" (Genesis 18:17-18).

Keep this foundational promise in mind as you read through the Pentateuch (and the whole Bible, for that matter). See how Yahweh works to be faithful to the promise in spite of human failure.

In the process of this interplay between God's promise and faithfulness compared with human action, the Pentateuch will include three major kinds of material: 1) stories, 2) laws, and 3) instructions about and calls for worship. These will often alternate, and they are tied together in interesting ways. Of course, it will be easier for you to enjoy reading the stories than the law. But try to understand how and why they are intertwined.

In Genesis you will find primarily stories, first the beginnings and then the story of Abraham and his early descendants, culminating in the story of Joseph and the explanation for how Abraham's family ended up in Egypt. Exodus takes up centuries later with the story of Moses and the exodus from Egypt. This is the great symbol of God's gracious salvation in the Old Testament. It then follows the people to Sinai, where Yahweh makes the covenant with them, gives them instruction on how to live and how to build a place where He will meet with them. These instructions include the Ten Commandments, which are seen as a response to God's grace revealed in the exodus. That is why the Ten Commandments begin with a brief prologue, which we too often ignore:

> "Then God spoke all these words: I am the Lord your God, who brought you out of the land of Egypt, out of the house of slavery; you shall have no other gods before me (Exodus 20:1-3).

Exodus also includes the story of Israel's first major failure to live up to the covenant.

Leviticus consists primarily of laws, instructions about sacrifice, and the way to observe the major feasts such as Passover, Weeks, Trumpets, and Booths. At the center of the book, in chapter 16, we find the Day of Atonement, showing its centrality. Numbers follows Israel through the wandering in the wilderness, and Deuteronomy records sermons Moses gives before his death, as well as the death itself. There is a definite pattern in these instructions: if you follow Yahweh and keep the covenant, it will go well with you; if you don't, it won't.

Some final tips: when you read the stories, be aware of the theological content and see what they tell you about God. But also enjoy them as stories. Remember that in ancient times there was no TV to watch or theater to attend, and these stories were not only instruction but also entertainment. Imagine people sitting around the fire at night and hearing these stories of their forebears. Look for all the good things that make up an entertaining story, such as plot, suspense, an unexpected turn of events, surprises, and irony. As mentioned earlier, my favorite story in the Pentateuch is one of the great sagas of ancient literature, the story of Joseph in Genesis 37-50. It has all of these elements and more. Think how delightful, entertaining, and inspiring it would have been to listen to such a story for the first time as you sat together with your neighbors.

When you read it, pay special attention to the following "bookends" that envelope the story.

Genesis 37:4 (speaking of the brothers in relationship to Joseph): "But when his brothers saw that their father loved him more than all his brothers, they hated him, and could not speak peaceably to him."

Genesis 50:20-21 (Joseph speaks to his brothers after the death of Jacob): "But Joseph said to them, 'Do not be afraid! Am I in the place of God? Even though you intended to do harm to me, God intended it for good, in order to preserve a numerous people, as he is doing today. So have no fear; I myself will provide for you and your little ones.' In this way he reassured them, speaking kindly to them."

When you think of these bookends, it is impossible to avoid the ethical challenge of this remarkable story.

We have to admit that much of the *torah* is not as much fun as the Joseph story. It will be easy to get bogged down when reading through the laws, but try to think about what God was trying to do for this community. Are there laws here that make perfect sense even today? Are there laws that seem very strange to us today? Can you try to imagine why God might have given such laws? What kind of community would such laws produce? Can you find enduring principles within even the laws that seem most distant from our reality? Finally, what do you learn about God as you read through the history of these encounters between God and the people of Israel?

For the Individual

1. Read the story of Isaac and Rebekah in Genesis 24. Then consider the following questions:

    a. How would you rate this as a story? Is it a good one? What kinds of story-telling devices do you find in the chapter? Do you find elements of suspense, surprise, irony, etc.? Do you think there would have been entertainment value to those who heard the story in Old Testament times?

    b. How would you evaluate the theology of the story? Do you learn anything about God from the story?

    c. Can you find areas where you resonate with the story emotionally, even though it comes from such a totally different cultural setting?

    d. Try to put yourself in the story. With whom do you identify in the story? Why?

2. Read Leviticus 1 and try to put yourself among those who brought sacrifices to the sanctuary, or later the temple, to sacrifice. Then consider the following questions.

    a. Can you imagine how you would have experienced sacrifice? What emotions might have been stirred? Would they have been primarily positive or negative?

    b. Can you understand why God would have given these instructions? Can you imagine why the prophets were so critical of sacrifice? How do you put these two together?

For the Group

1. Compare notes on your responses to the two passages you read in the questions for the individual. Are you agreed for the most part, or did you have significantly different reactions? If different, how

do you explain the different reactions?

2. Read Deuteronomy 6 together. Here Moses speaks to the people before they enter the Promised Land.

   a. How much do you find in this chapter that is familiar from the New Testament?

   b. Discuss the relationship between success and obedience in this chapter. To what extent does this perspective tell the whole story of God's dealing with humans?

   c. What do you learn about the religious education of children in this chapter? Can you think of specific ways you might use these principles today?

3. Now read together a later portion of Moses' speech in Deuteronomy 9.

   a. Is Moses being too hard on the people by calling them a continually stiff-necked and rebellious people? How would you respond if your pastor preached a similar sermon with similar language to your congregation next week?

   b. What do you think about Moses arguing with God about why He should save the Israelites and not destroy them?

4. From the sampling of readings so far, can you imagine yourself truly enjoying reading the Pentateuch? Why or why not?

CHAPTER ELEVEN

Tips for Enjoying the Former Prophets (or Historical Books) Plus Chronicles

It seems strange for us to think of the historical books of the Old Testament as "prophets," but that is the designation they have traditionally received. All that we have said about reading stories and appreciating the plot twists, suspense, surprises, and interesting characters in previous chapters especially applies to this part of the Bible.

First, a brief review of the contents of the six books that make up this section of the Old Testament. The six books are Joshua, Judges, 1 and 2 Samuel, and 1 and 2 Kings. The last four books were probably originally one book, divided only because it was too long to fit on a single scroll. We are also considering 1 and 2 Chronicles in this chapter, even though it is not part of the "Prophets" section of the Hebrew Bible but is grouped with the "Writings." However, since it covers the same material as Samuel and Kings, it makes sense to preview it here.

The book of Joshua takes up from where the Pentateuch left off and covers the conquest of Canaan by the Israelites. After the stories of conquest, the land is divided among the tribes. And just as Deuteronomy ends with Moses addressing the people before his death, Joshua ends with Joshua addressing the people and calling for covenant renewal before his death. Judges follows by presenting the time when Israel was still nomadic and vulnerable in the land and God raised up leaders to lead and guide them. In these books, we see God working to create the people who were to represent Him and His ways to the world.

1 Samuel begins with the story of Samuel as leader of the people and the establishment of kingship in Israel. It follows the kingship of Saul and his activities in relationship with David, and it ends with Saul's death. 2 Samuel begins with David mourning Saul and becoming king. It ends shortly before David's death.

1 Kings begins with the death of David and the accession of Solomon to the throne. It includes the story of the division of Solomon's kingdom after his death when the nation split in two, with Jeroboam leading the 10 northern tribes of Israel and Rehoboam leading the two southern tribes of Judah. It ends with the reign of Ahab in the North. 2 Kings then follows through until the destruction of the 10 northern tribes by Assyria in 722 and the invasion of the southern kingdom of Judah by the Babylonians in 586.

1 Chronicles begins with a long genealogy that covers the first nine chapters. There are other long lists of names in other chapters of

the two volumes as well. 1 Chronicles 10 then moves from the death of Saul. The same history we see in Samuel and Kings then follows until 2 Chronicles ends with the Babylonian captivity and the promise of the return of the exiles under Cyrus.

Now a few tips for enjoying this section of the Bible. First, it will be helpful to remember the relative dating of the history of Israel from David on so that you have some kind of historical framework in which to place the events. A brief list follows at the end of this chapter that you might want to copy and keep with you as you read. It will help you make sense of what is happening and keep things straight between the two kingdoms.

Second, it is important to remember what God is trying to accomplish in choosing a people and setting them up in the land promised to them. In doing this, God had to work with people within the context of their culture and the mores, values, and ethos of their day. From the perspective of God's subsequent revelations, especially seen in Jesus, "the image of the invisible God" (Colossians 1:15), not everything we read in Israel's history would be God's ideal. We need to remember what the beginning of the book of Hebrews proclaims:

> "Long ago God spoke to our ancestors in many and various ways by the prophets, but in these last days he has spoken to us by a Son, whom he appointed heir of all things, through whom he also created the worlds. He is the reflection of God's glory and the exact imprint of God's very being" (Hebrews 1:1-3).

It is the God revealed by Jesus who is acting in these stories. That is clear from the New Testament. This does not mean, however, that everything in God's interaction with His people and the surrounding nations, whose ways were often so opposed to God's ways, expresses His ideal. God has to work within the culture and understanding of the people.

This is a very honest history in so many ways. Even the heroes are seen with plenty of flaws and foibles. Observe how God works in spite of these foibles to accomplish the goal of creating the people and placing them in the land. Again we see how God remains faithful in spite of human failure.

When reading Joshua, notice the number of times events happen that explain the reasons for names and practices to future generations. Also notice the emphasis on how God keeps the promises made to Israel. How many of these do you see throughout the book? Also keep track of the number of times the book emphasizes that by placing Israel in Canaan and giving them the land, God is giving them "rest." Why do you think this idea of rest is so important? How does it contrast with their life wandering in the desert?

The book of Judges has so many incredibly interesting stories, although many of them would hardly be rated G or even PG if they were made into movies today. Think of how the first hearers of these stories would have been entertained, as well as instructed and inspired by God's action in the stories. These stories have a definite pattern to them. Look for the pattern as you read. They begin with the people turning away from Yahweh and then receiving punishment. A period of oppression follows. Finally the people wise up and repent. Then Yahweh raises up a leader, one of the judges, to help them. Then there is a period of peace until the next turning away. See how many times you can see this repeated pattern.

It is interesting to see that these judges or leaders that God raised up were not all men. In fact, try to take note throughout this book of how many times women seem to outdo men when it comes to responsibility and even bravery.

The book of Judges has a clear perspective that Israel needs a king. Without a king, everyone does what is right in their own eyes and things turn out to be a mess. In fact, the book ends with these words:

> "In those days there was no king in Israel; all the people did what was right in their own eyes" (Judges 21:25).

When we move on to the book of 1 Samuel, the perspective changes. Then we see the dangers of having a king. When the people insist that Samuel give them a king, it is seen as rebellion not only against Samuel but also against God (1 Samuel 8:7). Samuel goes on to warn them of all the terrible results of having a king:

> "These will be the ways of the king who will reign over you: he will take your sons and appoint them to his chariots and to be his horsemen, and to run before his chariots; and he will appoint for himself commanders of thousands and commanders of fifties, and some to plow his ground and to reap his harvest, and to make his implements of war and the equipment of his chariots. He will take your daughters to be perfumers and cooks and bakers. He will take the best of your fields and vineyards and olive orchards and give them to his courtiers. He will take one-tenth of your grain and of your vineyards and give it to his officers and his courtiers. He will take your male and female slaves, and the best of your

cattle and donkeys, and put them to his work. He will take one-tenth of your flocks, and you shall be his slaves. And in that day you will cry out because of your king, whom you have chosen for yourselves; but the Lord will not answer you in that day" (1 Samuel 8:11-18).

As you read Samuel and Kings, think about this dilemma—king or no king? Chaos or oppression? Notice how it plays out in Israel's history. Keep track of how many kings are good kings and how many kings are bad kings. And are the good ones all good and the bad ones all bad? Samuel and Kings tell the story of God leading and being faithful, both through Israel's kingship and in spite of Israel's kingship. Watch and see which factors lead to the success of the nation and which ones lead to times of difficulty and finally downfall. How do you assess the history of the kingdom period of Israel and its kings?

You will also enjoy the stories of Elijah (1 Kings 17 to 2 Kings 2) and Elisha (1 Kings 19 to 2 Kings 3) in Kings. Notice how there are events and miracles in Elisha's experience that mirror those of Elijah. As you read about Elijah in Kings, you might want to use a concordance to discover the role that Elijah plays in the New Testament.

1 and 2 Chronicles cover much the same ground as Samuel and Kings, but from a much later perspective. This two-volume work is much more concerned with genealogy, showing the records of the histories of the families and clans of Israel. It also presents a more positive picture of the history and of the kings. There is much less about the negative actions. For example, both 1 Kings 10 and 2 Chronicles 9 report the Queen of Sheba's visit to Solomon. The accounts are very similar. After this account, however, 1 Kings 11 goes on to show the

failures of Solomon and his turning away from God to the worship of foreign gods. But you won't find a hint of this in Chronicles. As you read through Samuel/Kings and Chronicles, see how many cases you find where the former presents negative elements that are not included in the latter.

Finally, think about how this history plays out in relationship to God. How might you compare and contrast this with what you see in government, political, and religious institutions today? What do you think we might learn from our reading of the history of Israel?

HISTORICAL FRAMEWORK FOR THE KINGS
OF ISRAEL AND JUDAH

United Kingdom
Saul (1050-1011)
David (1011-971)
Solomon (971-931)

Divided Kingdom

Northern Kingdom of Israel	Southern Kingdom of Judah
Jeroboam (931-910)	Rehoboam (931-913)
Nadab (910-909)	Abijah (913-911)
Baasha (909-886)	Asa (911-869)
Elah (886-885)	Jehoshaphat (872-848)
Zimri (885)	Jehoram (854-841)
Omri (885-874)	Ahaziah (841)
[Tibni (885-880]	Athaliah (841-835)
Ahab (874-853)	Joash (835-796)
Ahaziah (853-852)	Amaziah (796-767)
Jehoram (852-841)	Azariah (700-739)
Jehu (841-814)	Jotham (750-731)
Jehoahaz (814-798)	Ahaz (735-715)
Jehoash (798-782)	Hezekiah (729-686)
Jeroboam II (793-753)	Manasseh (696-641)
Zechariah (753-752)	Amon (641-639)
Shallum (752)	Josiah (639-608)
Menahem (752-742)	Jehoahaz II (608)
Pekahiah (742-740)	Jehoiakim (608-597)
Pekah (752-732)	Jehoiachin (597)
Hoshea (732-722)	Zedekiah (597-586)
Destruction by Assyria in 722	Destruction by Babylon in 586

Note: Many of these dates are disputed. Different lists will give different specifics, but this will give the reader a general picture of the flow of history during this period. This list is taken from the *Seventh-day Adventist Bible Commentary*, volume 2, page 77.

For the Individual

1. Read Judges 4 and 5, the story of the judge Deborah.

    a. How do you respond at an emotional level to the violence in this story? How do you explain the violence? Why is it there?

    b. Characterize each of the main players in the story. What do you like and dislike about each? How does God relate to each one?

    c. Explain the significance of the words in 4:9 that the honor would not go to Barak but to a woman. What would this have meant in their culture? What might it suggest now?

    d. Use an atlas to follow where the events of these chapters take place. Does this help illuminate the story for you?

    e. Compare and contrast the prose version of the story in chapter 4 and the poetic version of the story in chapter 5. Do they reveal the same picture? Could you make sense out of the poetic version without the prose version? What are the advantages and disadvantages of each version?

2. Scan through 2 Kings 8:16 to 25:30 (the end of the book) and take note of the kings of Israel and Judah.

    a. Do you find more good or bad kings? Is it the same for both countries?

    b. How does the stance of the king affect the nation as a whole? Do these stories suggest anything about the significance of leadership?

    c. What do you learn from God's response to both good and bad kings?

3. Have you found devotional value in these readings? If so, how?

For the Group

1. Share and compare your answers and reactions to the story of

Deborah in Judges 4 and 5. Have someone read the poetic version of the story in Judges 5. Do you experience the story differently when hearing it orally as opposed to reading it? Why do you think both versions are in the Bible?

2. Discuss the use of "good" and "bad" kings in 2 Kings.

   a. Do you think any of these kings were all good or all bad? Are leaders today either all good or all bad?

   b. If God is in control over the affairs of the world, why did He allow so many bad kings to reign?

3. What spiritual value can you find in reading these stories of the judges and kings of Israel and Judah?

CHAPTER TWELVE

Tips for Enjoying the Latter Prophets

Fifteen books make up this section of the Hebrew Bible. There are three major prophets—Isaiah, Jeremiah, and Ezekiel—who were the authors of lengthy books. Smaller books, written by the so-called minor prophets include Hosea, Joel, Amos, Obadiah, Jonah, Micah, Nahum, Habakkuk, Zephaniah, Haggai, Zechariah, and Malachi.

For ancient Israel and Judah, the term *prophet* meant something quite different from our typical, person-on-the-street understanding. We think of a prophet as someone who predicts the future. They thought of a prophet as one who spoke for God and addressed the people of God in His name. They challenged the people with a word from Yahweh.

Even when we think of the books of the Bible, we often think of the word *prophet* differently than it was used in these prophetic books. People today often use the word to refer to books like Daniel and Revelation, which use symbolic language to talk about the ultimate end of all things. A more appropriate term for those books, however, is *apocalyptic*, or an unveiling of God's reality that is not evident to us. Although some apocalyptic elements appear in the prophetic writings, they generally address God's will for His people here and now. These prophets wrote during the period of history covered by the books of Kings, the exile to Babylon, and the return from exile. They addressed not only God's people but the surrounding nations as well with a word from Yahweh. Since the prophetic oracles from God give both warnings and promises that are dependent on the people's response, not all of the judgment scenarios envisioned actually occurred. (See the book of Jonah, for instance.)

Much of what they wrote, as you will see if you read in a contemporary translation, was in poetic form. Although each of the prophets had his own unique message, there are several major concerns that these prophets share.

One of the most important is social justice. The prophets show great concern for the poor, oppressed, widows, and orphans. They are especially angered by the juxtaposition of supposed piety and disregard for people in need. For the prophets, worship without justice and ethical responsibility is not only vacuous, it is the epitome of evil. The prophets speak for God to those in power on behalf of the oppressed. The prophets are keen to expose the abuse of power among all leaders, whether kings or priests. Although several of the prophets come from among the priests, they are concerned about the priestly cult when it fails to seek justice.

Of equal concern among the prophets was idolatry. Whenever God's people turned to foreign gods and participated in their cultic worship, the prophets took aim. Of course, most worship of these foreign gods involved rituals that had to do with fertility and involved various forms of sexual immorality. The prophets demanded unyielding commitment to Yahweh and no other god. A good portion of the message of the prophets focused in one way or another on these two concerns: idolatry and social injustice.

The prophets used a number of literary conventions to convey their messages. Most of the messages came in certain forms of speech that we see repeated in the various prophets. They also make use of colorful speech that includes analogies, metaphors, wordplay, and audio-visual aids. Here are some of the major kinds of forms of prophetic speech that you will want to look for as you read, which will enhance your ability to follow what the prophet is trying to say.

The most frequent is the prophetic oracle, in which the prophet gives a poetic word from Yahweh. There are several kinds of oracles. There is the oracle of salvation, in which the prophet presents a positive message about what Yahweh, in His unending faithfulness, will do for the people. These often come in times of trouble and promise God's continuing presence and restoration. In contrast, however, there is the oracle of doom that warns of sure and certain judgment for those who have turned away from Yahweh and/or have perpetrated violence and injustice. Somewhere between these two is the woe oracle, which offers warning but also the possibility of repentance, reversal, and restoration.

Other forms include the oracle against the foreign nations. These probably were used as Israel went to war against these nations or was threatened by them. In these, Yahweh shows His authority over not only Israel but also the other nations as well, for Yahweh is more powerful than their gods. We find hymns, frequent in the Psalms, in the prophets as well. Here God's people are called to praise and are given reason for the praise. There are vision reports that reveal what Yahweh has shown the prophet. Sometimes Yahweh's message is in the form of a legal charge, where God brings a legal case against the people for their transgressions. The prophets also use various forms of prophetic symbolic actions, often commanded by God. Hosea is commanded to marry a prostitute (Hosea 1-3). Jeremiah is commanded to buy a worthless piece of property (Jeremiah 32). Isaiah is told to preach naked and barefoot (Isaiah 20). Ezekiel is commanded to lie on his left side for 390 days and on his right for 40 (Ezekiel 4). These commands may seem bizarre, but they certainly made the prophetic messages graphic.

You will enjoy reading these books much more, and you will understand them better as well, if you pay attention to these various forms that the prophets used to convey Yahweh's message. And as you enjoy and understand, you should also hear God's voice challenging us today in our culture just as He challenged the ancient culture. Although within the scope of this work we cannot go into detail, here are a few random tips for reading each of the 15 books of the latter prophets. We will go through them in roughly chronological order, although the time of writing is not clear for Joel and Jonah. The eighth century produced Amos, Hosea, Isaiah, and Micah.

Amos

Notice how Amos begins his eighth century message with God's judgment against the nations who are Israel's neighbors. Damascus,

Gaza, Tyre, Edom, Ammon, and Moab are all rebuked. Then there is a brief pronouncement of judgment on Judah, the southern part of David's kingdom. By this time readers in Israel might be cheering Amos on. But then he turns the tables, and the rest of the book focuses on Israel, the northern kingdom whose capital was in Samaria (although there are other statements of Judah's sin in the book as well). Her sins are recounted one by one. Pay attention to what these sins are. How many are specifically religious or theological? How many are social or political? The ancient Israelites probably wouldn't have made this kind of distinction, of course. As you outline the reasons for judgment, how many might apply to our cultures today? Notice what Amos says about Israel's worship and sacrifice. Chapter 5 offers a lament in advance for Israel's fall. Notice the context of the most famous verse in the book, Amos 5:24:

> "But let justice roll down like waters,
>   and righteousness like an ever-flowing stream."

To what extent was the use of this text in the American civil rights movement consistent with the message and context of Amos? Notice that the only hint of hope and restoration comes at the very end. Some have argued that this conclusion of the book was added later to keep Amos' message from being quite so stark. Why might they think this? What do you think?

Pay attention to the concept of *the day of the Lord* in Amos. Apparently the people used the term for a hopeful day of salvation, but Amos turns the tables and says:

> "Alas for you who desire the day of the Lord!

Why do you want the day of the Lord?
It is darkness, not light" (Amos 5:18).

You will get more out of the message of chapter 8 if you understand a wordplay Amos employs. He sees a basket of summer fruit
and then goes on to talk about "the end." In English there is no connection here, but in Hebrew the word for *summer fruit* is *qits* and for
end is *qets*. Finally, let this book help you reflect on what it means for
God to be a God of justice.

Hosea

The book of Hosea portrays idolatry as spiritual adultery against
Yahweh. Israel entered into a covenant to be faithful to Yahweh, and
by going after other gods she breaks this sacred vow. (Keep in mind
that the northern kingdom can also be called Samaria, after its capital, or Ephraim, after its largest tribe.) This adultery is graphically il-
lustrated by the real-life experience of Hosea, who is commanded to
marry a prostitute and be faithful to her in spite of her unfaithfulness
to him. Notice the names given to the children of Gomer's unfaithfulness. Try to imagine the scene in the household and what it would
mean for children to carry these names around with them. Does this
image still speak today? It might be interesting to use a concordance
and see how these names, like *not my people*, appear in the messages
of New Testament writers.

See if you can find other metaphors for God's love that are related to family life throughout Hosea. Compare the sins recounted in
Hosea with those Amos was concerned about. Also keep track of the
many different similes and metaphors that Hosea uses throughout
the book. Try to keep track of different forms of speech and literary

devices Hosea uses. One of these is the lawsuit or indictment God brings against Israel. Notice the back and forth interplay between judgment and promises of restoration. How would you compare the portrait of God in this book with that of Amos?

Isaiah

The greatest of the eighth century prophets is Isaiah, whose focus is on the southern kingdom of Judah. There is much debate about the unity and authorship of Isaiah. Such questions are beyond the scope of this volume, but see if you notice a marked difference in the material in chapters 1 to 39 as compared with chapters 40 to 66. These latter chapters at least address a different situation. While the first part of the book addresses the issues of the eighth century, the latter chapters seek to give comfort to the Jews who have been carried off to Babylon in the sixth century.

In addition to other forms we have mentioned, Isaiah includes the prophetic call (see Isaiah 6). We will see this in some of the other prophets as well. What do you see as the basic elements of this call? How does it compare and contrast with other call narratives you encounter in the Bible? (You might compare the calls of Jeremiah in Jeremiah 1 or Paul in Acts 9.)

Notice how Isaiah's family plays a role in his prophetic ministry; as was the case for Hosea, the names of Isaiah's children play a role in the story. See if you can find other prophetic forms in Isaiah, such as oracles of salvation, oracles against the nations, vision reports, divine lawsuits against the people, laments, hymns, and songs. How does Isaiah use these various patterns to convey his message? How does his message compare and contrast with Amos and Hosea?

In the latter part of the book, try to keep track of the different ways God tries to comfort a discouraged, exiled people. Notice how metaphors of family also play a role here. In fact, you might want to look for places where God uses feminine images, such as mothering, to convey love for the people.

Although Isaiah included oracles against the nations (chapters 13 to 23), see if you can find visions of inclusiveness in Isaiah. Are there places where God speaks of embracing the other nations and bringing them together with Israel? The apostle Paul seemed to think so. He makes significant use of Isaiah in Romans when he argues for the inclusion of the Gentiles in the community of Christ. And as you read through the passages about a servant who suffers in Isaiah 50 to 53, try and see if you can make sense out of what this would have meant for people in Isaiah's day. Why do you think these chapters became so important to early Christians, and how did the message of these chapters relate to their experience with Jesus as the Messiah?

Micah

Notice that at the outset Micah addresses both the northern and southern kingdoms, naming their capitals, both Samaria and Jerusalem. He utilizes all the forms of prophetic speech that appear in the other prophets, and he certainly graphically presents the messages of justice and faithfulness to Yahweh that we see in most of the prophets. Here are some specifics you might look for in Micah. Observe how he singles out the leaders of the people for rebuke. What do you learn about the role and influence of leadership from Micah? Watch also for the interplay between judgment on the one hand and restoration and promise on the other. The promises in Micah are especially vivid. Can you see how early Christians saw that so much of what Micah says was fulfilled in Jesus as the Messiah?

Finally, the most familiar verse in Micah, Micah 6:8, summarizes what God requires of humans. Note the context of this passage. What contrast is Micah making? How would you define in today's culture what it means to do justice, love mercy, and walk humbly with God?

Nahum

We now move to prophets of the seventh century: Nahum, Zephaniah, Jeremiah, and Habakkuk. We will include the two prophets whose dates are uncertain here as well: Jonah and Joel. Nahum is a short work of only three chapters and is primarily an oracle against the nations, in this case Nineveh. The denunciations of judgment on Nineveh, the capital of the powerful Assyrian kingdom, are vivid and unequivocal. However, look for what God says on the positive side about His own people. Interspersed throughout the oracle against Nineveh are oracles of salvation for Judah.

Jonah

Although the dating of Jonah is uncertain, it makes sense to read it beside Nahum because of the content. While Nahum presents God's uncompromising judgment on Nineveh, Jonah makes a case that God loves and cares for the inhabitants of Nineveh. It might be good to spend some time thinking about how you put these two messages together.

Jonah is another great Hebrew story. While most of the prophetic books are poetry, except for the prayers, Jonah is prose. The book is full of irony and surprising plot twists. Notice the different movement in each of the chapters, as Jonah runs from God, remembers God, preaches God's message, and then complains to God about the success of his preaching.

Ask yourself to what extent Jonah's attitude is like the message of the book of Nahum. How is the perspective of the presumably anonymous narrator of the Jonah story different from the perspectives of Nahum or Jonah? How do you account for this?

Pay attention to the end of the book. What is the role of the bush, the tree, the hot wind, and the animals? Also notice the similarity between the beginnings of chapters 1 and 3, and then again between chapters 2 and 4. Also compare and contrast Jonah's attitude with that of the various foreigners who appear in the book. It is hard not to enjoy this book. That's why it is a favorite of children when they learn Bible stories. But it is also a profound challenge to the exclusivism of those who think God is only on their side, whether in ancient Judah or today.

Habakkuk

Habakkuk had a problem with God. Why didn't God do something about the violence and injustice so prevalent among God's own people in Habakkuk's day? The answer God gave was unacceptable to Habakkuk, and he didn't mind telling God so. God says He's sending Babylon to bring judgment. But Habakkuk knows the Babylonians are even worse than Judah, so how can this possibly be an appropriate answer to his question? Pay close attention to this fascinating dialogue between God and Habakkuk. Try to differentiate between God's words and those of Habakkuk. What might this dialogue suggest about prayer? Then see Habakkuk's attitude in the third chapter. How do you understand Habakkuk's prayer in this chapter? What leads him to this kind of trust?

Pay particular attention to chapter 2, verse 4:

"Look at the proud!

> Their spirit is not right in them,
> but the righteous live by their faith."

What does Habakkuk mean by this? What makes this such an important text for Paul in Romans?

Jeremiah

Jeremiah is one of the most interesting prophets. Like Habakkuk, he was not at all afraid to shake his fist at God, complain, and argue. He was given one of the most difficult tasks of any prophet. Can you imagine having to tell the people of your nation, God's own people, that God was going to bring judgment on them and their only hope was to surrender to their worst enemy, the Babylonians, as a sign of their obedience and repentance. (When Jeremiah refers to disaster coming from the North, he is referring to Babylon.) It's hardly surprising that Jeremiah blames God for tricking him into a situation where he is persecuted if he does preach (going to prison, being thrown into a pit, friends trying to kill him) and condemned and guilty before God if he doesn't. (See the beginning of chapter 20.) He says it would have been better if he had never been born.

These sections where Jeremiah complains to God are called the "confessions" of Jeremiah. Watch for these sections as you read through the book. You will see lots of raw emotions, including anger, loneliness, discouragement, and at times even joy. Here is one example of these "confessions."

> "Cursed be the day
>   on which I was born!
> The day when my mother bore me,

let it not be blessed!
Cursed be the man
   who brought the news to my father, saying,
'A child is born to you, a son,'
   making him very glad.
Let that man be like the cities
   that the Lord overthrew without pity;
let him hear a cry in the morning
   and an alarm at noon,
because he did not kill me in the womb;
   so my mother would have been my grave,
   and her womb forever great.
Why did I come forth from the womb
   to see toil and sorrow,
   and spend my days in shame?" (Jeremiah 20:14-18).

There is a lot more biographical information about Jeremiah in the book than for most of the other prophets. Unfortunately, the material is somewhat disjointed, so you might need to take some notes to keep up with it.

In fact, much of the book of Jeremiah skips around historically. This is probably due to subsequent editing of Jeremiah's message. In the Septuagint, the Greek translation of the Hebrew Old Testament, the order of the material is quite different.

You will find most of the common prophetic speeches in Jeremiah—oracles of judgment, oracles against the nations, and especially judgment on God's people, Judah. As in Isaiah, there is a call narrative that shows Jeremiah's reluctance from the very beginning. Apparently he was quite young when called.

You will also want to look for the many symbolic prophetic actions Jeremiah performs at God's command, including visiting a potter's house, not marrying, wearing a yoke, and tossing a book into the Euphrates River. Jeremiah is nothing if not vivid, and this adds interest to the reading.

Pay special attention to Jeremiah's ultimate faithfulness and commitment to God in spite of incredibly difficult circumstances. See if you can find answers within the book that account for Jeremiah's ability to stick with it. Also notice how, in spite of giving a message that is primarily about judgment, we see striking moments of Jeremiah's compassion for the people—and of God's compassion as well.

As you reach the end of the book, see how the tables are turned and there is judgment against Babylon as well. Even though Babylon is the agent of God's judgment, that doesn't free her from responsibility for her violent actions. Also at the end of the book you will find a historical description of the destruction of Jerusalem.

Jeremiah is a long book, and there is a lot of judgment and denunciation to wade through, but there is also a fascinating story of a prophet with an impossible task whose open and honest communication with God keeps him faithful through it all.

Zephaniah

In this brief, three-chapter work by another seventh-century prophet, notice the movement from judgment on Judah, to judgment on the nations, back to Judah, then back to the nations. Notice also how Zephaniah, like Amos, warns that the hoped-for day of the Lord would be bad news, not good news. But then look at the final song of hope, joy, restoration, and redemption. How does this brief work sum up the message of the prophets?

Joel

The dating of the book of Joel is not certain, but the specific background is. A locust plague has come, and the prophet uses it as a symbol of the approaching judgment to come if God's people do not repent. No prophet portrays coming judgment with more vivid details. Yet as is typical of the prophets, there is also hope if the people will repent, for God is compassionate. In Joel 2:12-14 there is hope:

> "Yet even now, says the Lord,
>   return to me with all your heart,
> with fasting, with weeping, and with mourning;
>   rend your hearts and not your clothing.
> Return to the Lord, your God,
>   for he is gracious and merciful,
> slow to anger, and abounding in steadfast love,
>   and relents from punishing.
> Who knows whether he will not turn and relent,
>   and leave a blessing behind him?"

Joel gives hope for Judah's restoration and proclaims that the nations that torment her will be brought down. Take special note of Joel 2:28-29 and see how it is used by Peter in Acts 2 at Pentecost.

Ezekiel

Ezekiel and Obadiah were written during the Babylonian exile. Ezekiel is another of the three major prophets. Reading Ezekiel is anything but boring. In this book you will find strange winged animals with multiple faces; wheels in wheels; scrolls that are eaten; hair that is shaved from the prophet's head, with part of it being burned;

dry, dead bones that rattle, gather together, and live again; and detailed descriptions of a new temple that never actually existed as described. Some of what we see in Ezekiel is nothing less than bizarre.

In Ezekiel we see the same threefold message as in Zephaniah: judgment on Judah, judgment on the nations, and restoration for Judah. But instead of three chapters, there are 48. The first 24 focus the judgments on God's people (although there are promises of restoration interspersed within this material), while chapters 25 to 32 focus on the other nations. The last 16 chapters have mostly to do with restoration.

In Ezekiel, however, there are many unique elements in addition to these common prophetic motifs. Ezekiel is a priest, and there is more concern with ritual, issues of clean and unclean, and the restoration of the temple. Ezekiel differs from most of the prophets by writing in the first person through most of the book. There are many vivid analogies and illustrations. And although God commands several of the prophets to perform symbolic events in their lives to illustrate the message (Hosea marrying a prostitute, Isaiah going naked), this happens much more in Ezekiel. Ezekiel is told that he cannot mourn when his wife dies, for instance. The book of Ezekiel may confuse us at times, but it is always interesting. And it is hard not to be inspired by the vivid pictures of God's promised restoration through images such as the dry bones coming to life. Another beautiful image of restoration depicts the glory of God leaving the temple in chapter 10, and then the return of God's glory to the temple in chapter 43. Be sure and read both of these chapters carefully to see the movement from judgment to restoration. Finally, see if you don't find in Ezekiel elements that almost seem more like the apocalyptic books of Daniel and Revelation than the other latter prophets.

Obadiah

Obadiah, like Nahum, is primarily an announcement of judgment on a single nation, in this case the nation of Edom. According to tradition, the Edomites were the descendants of Esau, Jacob or Israel's brother. But when the Babylonians came to capture God's people, the Edomites didn't act very brotherly. This tiny book of one chapter condemns them and promises that Israel will be restored.

Haggai

The final three prophets come from post-exilic times, when at least some of the captives have returned to Jerusalem. The short, two-chapter book of Haggai carries a very specific message. The people have returned and are living in fine houses, but they have not rebuilt the temple. It is time for them to bring their funds and materials and build, with the added caveat that in order to do the work the people have to be right with God as well. The book usually appears only in stewardship sermons. Do you think the book could be useful in other ways as well?

Zechariah

This prophetic book from the latter part of the sixth century speaks to the remnant of exiles who have returned to Jerusalem about rebuilding the temple, but in contrast to Haggai, who is much more straightforward, it does so with symbolic visions that remind us of Ezekiel and can seem bizarre. Look for what God is trying to get the exiles to do, both in rebuilding the temple and in forming a community of justice that would attract other nations to come and find Yahweh. Notice also the importance of leadership and God's concern and promises for the leaders. Had you lived in this time of return from exile, would you have been encouraged by these visions and by the promises that those who had fought against them and taken them captive would receive their due? Try to see if Zechariah gives you enough explanation of the visions to allow you to figure out what he is trying to say. You will also find a number of references in Zechariah that reappear in the life and ministry of Jesus. Within the context of the original readers, do you think these were specific predictions about Christ?

Malachi

This interesting post-exilic prophet presents a series of arguments between God and the people. God makes a statement, then the people argue, and finally God shows why the charge against them is true and their attempted rebuttal falls short. Look at what God says, then see how the people respond and how God responds to their argument. Here are some of the things God says about them:

I have loved you.
Your priests show contempt for my name.
Judah has been unfaithful.
You have wearied me with your words.
You are robbing me in tithes and offerings.
You have spoken arrogantly about me.

See how the people argue with God and how God responds. How many of these issues might still be issues today? Finally, think about the references to Moses and Elijah at the end of the book. How are these final words of the Old Testament relevant for the New Testament?

For the Individual

1. Read the book of Micah, and, if you can, listen to it read orally as well.

   a. What prophetic forms do you see in Micah? Do you find examples of oracles of judgment, oracles of salvation, woes, legal cases against the people, etc.? Which forms are the most prevalent?

   b. How do you make sense out of the contrasting messages of judgment and salvation?

   c. What are some of the metaphors, similes, and figures of speech that Micah uses? How do these enliven Micah's message?

   d. What does Micah have to say about leaders such as prophets and priests? Why does he focus so much attention on them?

   e. Is Micah's main concern about the people's idolatry and turning from God, or about their treatment of other people? How does Micah relate the two?

   f. What do you find in Micah that was used in the New Testament to refer to Jesus? How would these references have been understood by the original readers?

2. Of the 15 books found among the prophets in the Hebrew Bible, which is your favorite and why?

For the Group

1. Compare and contrast your answers to the questions about Micah in the section for individuals.

   a. Discuss whether or not you like reading Micah. What do you find about the book that is intriguing, inspiring, puzzling, spiritually beneficial, practically helpful, etc.?

   b. From the context of the book as a whole, what does it mean to act justly, love mercy, and walk humbly with God?

   c. What do you learn about worship from this book?

2. Discuss the concept of prophet. What is the role of the prophet? Has your study of this book changed your understanding of the prophetic role?

CHAPTER THIRTEEN

Tips for Enjoying the Writings

The final section of the Hebrew Bible is diverse indeed. It includes historical works such as 1 and 2 Chronicles (which we have already covered), Ezra, and Nehemiah; poetic songs such as Psalms, Lamentations, and Song of Songs; wisdom literature such as Job, Proverbs, and Ecclesiastes; the apocalyptic book of Daniel; and stories such as Ruth and Esther. Five of these books were grouped together in a section called the *megilloth*, or "little scrolls." They are Ruth, Esther, Song of Songs, Ecclesiastes, and Lamentations. The largest and probably most loved of the works in this section of the Bible is the Psalms, so let's begin there.

Psalms

Psalms is not only the largest work in this section of the Bible, it is the largest book of the entire Bible. This collection of songs was Israel's hymnbook for worship. It continued to be well loved by the early Christians as well. There are more than 400 references to the Old Testament in the New Testament, and over 40 percent of them are from the Psalms. There are 150 psalms in this collection, and they are divided into five sections as follows:

Book 1 (Psalms 1-41)

Book 2 (Psalms 42-72)

Book 3 (Psalms 73-89)

Book 4 (Psalms 90-106)

Book 5 (Psalms 107-150)

Each section ends with a call to praise. The second book ends by saying that this ends the prayers of David.

Although we generally think of David as the author of the psalms, the superscriptions at the beginnings of the psalms list other names as well. It is not clear whether in each case these superscriptions are always statements of authorship. From the content it is clear that Israel's hymnbook was written over a period of centuries by various poets.

In order to enjoy the psalms fully, it is helpful to grasp something of the variety of types of psalms. Many of these types have a fairly set pattern that is repeated from psalm to psalm. Here are some of the major types of psalms and the patterns they follow.

The Hymn

The hymn is a call to praise. Many of the psalms are hymns, and they generally follow a pattern that begins with a command to praise, or sing, or shout for joy, etc. This is often followed by who is to follow the command and perhaps how they are to do it. Then there will be a transition, with the word *for*, followed by the reason for the command. Thus a pattern of:

What

Who

How

Why

The shortest example of a hymn (and the shortest of the psalms) is Psalm 117:

"Praise the Lord, all you nations!
    Extol him, all you peoples!
For great is his steadfast love toward us,
    and the faithfulness of the Lord endures forever.
Praise the Lord!"

Notice the pattern:

What: praise or extol the Lord

Who: all the nations or peoples

(The how is not present in this hymn)

Why: for His love is great and His faithfulness endures

Look for this pattern in many of the psalms, and when you see it, keep record of the reasons why God should be praised. See if this might enrich your own prayer life.

The Lament

This is the most frequent type of psalm in the book of Psalms. Like all humans, the psalmists had problems, and because they were believers they took these problems to God. Generally, the first part of the psalm focuses on the problem. There is an address to God, a statement of the problem, a complaint and plea to God, and often a bit of bargaining with God. The psalmist will often remind God, for example, that if God lets them die they won't be able to praise Him. The second part of the psalm focuses on the solution. First there is an expression of confidence that God will hear the prayer, followed by praise to God for hearing, and finally a statement of the expected result. An example of a lament psalm is found in Psalm 6. See how many of these elements you can find in this psalm (at least one is missing).

> "O Lord, do not rebuke me in your anger,
>> or discipline me in your wrath.
> Be gracious to me, O Lord, for I am languishing;
>> O Lord, heal me, for my bones are shaking with terror.
> My soul also is struck with terror,
>> while you, O Lord—how long?
> Turn, O Lord, save my life;
>> deliver me for the sake of your steadfast love.
> For in death there is no remembrance of you;
>> in Sheol who can give you praise?
> I am weary with my moaning;
>> every night I flood my bed with tears;
>> I drench my couch with my weeping.
> My eyes waste away because of grief;
>> they grow weak because of all my foes.
> Depart from me, all you workers of evil,
>> for the Lord has heard the sound of my weeping.

The Lord has heard my supplication;
>   the Lord accepts my prayer.
All my enemies shall be ashamed and struck with terror;
>   they shall turn back, and in a moment be put to shame."

There are two kinds of laments: individual and communal. This lament is an individual lament. Some laments speak not of a single person's problem but of one that confronts the entire nation, and the community laments together. There are some laments where there is no transition to resolution. It is all dark. Perhaps the best example is Psalm 88. The last word of the psalm is *darkness*.

Some wonder how psalms that are inspired by God can express such darkness. Perhaps God uses the honest feelings of these psalmists to teach us something about how to pray. It isn't that God inspired all the feelings expressed in the psalms, but He inspired the psalmist to bring these feelings to God in open, honest communication. Within the context of that kind of relationship, God was able to bring help and healing.

Imprecatory Psalms

These are undoubtedly the hardest for Christians to understand. These are psalms that lash out against "enemies." In fact, many psalms not in this category speak about enemies. There are two main words for *enemy* in Hebrew, and one or the other is used in over one third of all the psalms. Even the most famous psalm, the beautiful shepherd psalm of Psalm 23, seems to gloat at the end that the Lord feeds the psalmist with his enemies looking on. Some psalms can seem quite vicious. Psalm 137 begins with a poignant picture of those carried captive to Babylon, weeping for Jerusalem and vowing never to forget it. But it ends with these words about Babylon:

> "O daughter Babylon, you devastator!
>> Happy shall they be who pay you back
>> what you have done to us!
> Happy shall they be who take your little ones
>> and dash them against the rock!" (Psalm 137:8-9).

The psalms express every emotion that humans can experience: intense joy, devastating sorrow, vindictive anger, depressing despair, and any other emotion you can think of. In other words, the psalms are real. And that is what makes them so appealing. Wherever we are in our journey, we can find psalms that resonate with us and teach us how to express the depths of our souls to God. It is helpful not only to read the psalms but to pray through them and let them help you express yourself to God.

Wisdom or Instructional Psalms

Some of the psalms are much like the wisdom literature we will discuss later in this chapter. They give wise instruction to the believer. The very first psalm is a good example. Here are the first three verses:

> "Happy are those
>> who do not follow the advice of the wicked,
> or take the path that sinners tread,
>> or sit in the seat of scoffers;
> but their delight is in the law of the Lord,
>> and on his law they meditate day and night.
> They are like trees

planted by streams of water,
which yield their fruit in its season,
    and their leaves do not wither.
In all that they do, they prosper."

Penitential Psalms

These psalms speak of forgiveness. They anticipate the words of the Lord's Prayer, "And forgive us our debts, as we also have forgiven our debtors" (Matthew 6:12). Probably the most well known is Psalm 51, which begins:

"Have mercy on me, O God,
    according to your steadfast love;
according to your abundant mercy
    blot out my transgressions.
Wash me thoroughly from my iniquity,
    and cleanse me from my sin.
For I know my transgressions,
    and my sin is ever before me" (Psalm 51:1-3).

Royal Psalms

These psalms were probably used when Israel crowned a new king. One might think of Handel's *Coronation Anthems* used for the ceremonies crowning British monarchs. Christians, of course, can't read these psalms without thinking about Jesus as King of Kings, so it is not surprising that the New Testament makes use of these psalms to celebrate Jesus. The second psalm provides an example that is used often throughout the New Testament. In it, God warns the surrounding nations that the king of Israel is His anointed. The first few verses proclaim:

> "Why do the nations conspire,
>   and the peoples plot in vain?
> The kings of the earth set themselves,
>   and the rulers take counsel together,
>   against the Lord and his anointed, saying,
> 'Let us burst their bonds asunder,
>   and cast their cords from us.'
> He who sits in the heavens laughs;
>   the Lord has them in derision.
> Then he will speak to them in his wrath,
>   and terrify them in his fury, saying,
> 'I have set my king on Zion, my holy hill'" (Psalm 2:1-6).

Pilgrim Psalms

Psalms 120 to 134 form a unique collection of short psalms called "songs of ascent" that seem to have been sung by pilgrims on their way to Jerusalem for the annual feasts. They often sing of Zion or Jerusalem and have many references to family and nature. Here is one example, Psalm 122, in its entirety:

> "I was glad when they said to me,
>   'Let us go to the house of the Lord!'
> Our feet are standing
>   within your gates, O Jerusalem.
> Jerusalem—built as a city
>   that is bound firmly together.
> To it the tribes go up,

the tribes of the Lord,
as was decreed for Israel,
    to give thanks to the name of the Lord.
For there the thrones for judgment were set up,
    the thrones of the house of David.
Pray for the peace of Jerusalem:
    'May they prosper who love you.
Peace be within your walls,
    and security within your towers.'
For the sake of my relatives and friends
    I will say, 'Peace be within you.'
For the sake of the house of the Lord our God,
    I will seek your good."

This does not exhaust the kinds of psalms. There are also prophetic psalms that give a message much like that of the prophets. Psalm 50 is a good example. There are psalms of thanksgiving, which often overlap with the hymns of praise. These examples, however, give an idea of how diverse Israel's hymnbook really was, and this can provide a guide for reading through them. You will find virtually every human emotion represented here, from joy to sorrow, from hope to despair, from anger to love, from revenge to forgiveness. As you read through the psalms, take note of some of these and come back to them when you are experiencing these varying emotions, and pray with the psalmist. The psalms can be a tremendous tool for enhancing your prayer life.

There is one other aspect of the psalms that needs attention to enhance your enjoyment. It helps to understand a bit about how Hebrew poetry works. It does not utilize rhyme as some English poetry does. Here a few basic characteristics of Hebrew poetry.

Parallelism is the most common characteristic of the poetry you will find in the Old Testament. The psalmists and the prophets usually say something twice in different words. Notice how this occurs in that shortest of the psalms, which we have already viewed, Psalm 117.

> "Praise the Lord, all you nations!
>   Extol him, all you peoples!
> For great is his steadfast love toward us,
>   and the faithfulness of the Lord endures forever.
> Praise the Lord!"

The first two lines say the same thing with synonyms. *Praise* and *extol* are synonyms, as are *nations* and *peoples*. In the next two lines, *steadfast love* and *faithfulness* are also synonyms. You will find this over and over, until you come to expect it. However, the psalmists will often vary the parallelism by saying the opposite thing in the second line. For example, Psalm 1:6 reads:

> "for the Lord watches over the way of the righteous,
>   but the way of the wicked will perish."

Here the parallelism is opposite.

Sometimes the psalmists employ a chiastic structure using the form A, B, B, A. For example, in Psalm 51 quoted above, the first verse reads:

> A) Have mercy on me, O God,
> B) according to your steadfast love;

B) according to your abundant mercy

A) blot out my transgressions.

Some of the other poetic conventions are unfortunately only apparent in the original language. For instance, some psalmists make use of the acrostic. The most obvious example is Psalm 119, where each line of the first stanza begins with the first letter of the Hebrew alphabet, each line of the second stanza begins with the second letter, and so on throughout all 22 letters of the alphabet. Another device not visible to the English reader is alliteration. When Psalm 122:6 admonishes, "Pray for the peace of Jerusalem," the Hebrew is *sh-aalu shalom yerushalam*. Notice the repetition of the *sh* sound.

We have spent quite a bit of time on the Psalms, but this is, after all, the longest book of the Bible and certainly one of the most valuable for our devotional experience. Not only were the psalms central to the worship experience of Israel but, as their frequent use in the New Testament shows, they were vital to the earliest Christians as well. However, their influence in worship hardly stops there. A quick survey of virtually any Christian hymnal will show that much of our hymnody makes reference to the Psalms.

Proverbs

If I had written the book of Proverbs, it would have been written much differently. I would have grouped all the proverbs on a single theme together, so that all proverbs on the theme of money would have made up one section, all proverbs on the theme of family another, and all proverbs about work in another. But those who collected the proverbs didn't do that. They are all mixed in together without any apparent rhyme or reason. Perhaps part of that has to do with the nature of proverbs.

The wisdom literature of the sages represented in the Proverbs doesn't seek to give a coherent argument on a topic or to present ultimate truth. Rather it shares wisdom that gives guidance for life in certain kinds of situations. Yet because the proverbs give wise sayings about life in its various, complex settings, the proverbs often seem to contradict each other. We should expect that from proverbs. It is true of the traditional proverbs we find in our own English language and American culture. It almost seems that for every proverb there is an opposite proverb. For example, we say,

"Haste makes waste" and "Look before you leap."

But we also say,

"He who hesitates is lost."

We say,

"Many hands make light work."

But we also say,

"Too many cooks spoil the broth."

Since proverbs give conventional wisdom for different situations in life, it is inevitable, given the complexity of life, that they will give balance and advice to help us avoid both extremes. The Hebrew proverbs are no exception. On the one hand, Proverbs warns us against getting too involved in seeking for wealth:

"Do not wear yourself out to get rich;
be wise enough to desist.

When your eyes light upon it, it is gone;
  for suddenly it takes wings to itself,
  flying like an eagle toward heaven" (Proverbs 23:4-5).

On the other hand, it warns against getting too lazy:

"How long will you lie there, O lazybones?
  When will you rise from your sleep?
A little sleep, a little slumber,
  a little folding of the hands to rest,
and poverty will come upon you like a robber,
  and want, like an armed warrior" (Proverbs 6:9-11).

Sometimes proverbs that seem opposite can come sequentially one right after the other, as in Proverbs 26:4-5:

"Do not answer fools according to their folly,
  or you will be a fool yourself.
Answer fools according to their folly,
  or they will be wise in their own eyes."

Key words for understanding proverbs are wisdom, balance, and common sense.

The book of Proverbs is a collection of wise sayings covering many years. Actually, it is a collection of collections. We often think of them as all coming from Solomon, because he is mentioned in Proverbs 1:1 as the author, but when we read the whole collection we find other authors mentioned, such as Agur (Proverbs 30:1). Right at the beginning, the collection sets forth the purpose of proverbs:

"For learning about wisdom and instruction,
    for understanding words of insight,
for gaining instruction in wise dealing,
    righteousness, justice, and equity;
to teach shrewdness to the simple,
    knowledge and prudence to the young—
let the wise also hear and gain in learning,
    and the discerning acquire skill,
to understand a proverb and a figure,
    the words of the wise and their riddles" (Proverbs 1:2-6).

The first few chapters of Proverbs read like essays about the life of wisdom. Most of the rest of the book gives short, mostly two-line sayings in no apparent order. We know that some of these sayings are analogous to the wisdom of other peoples from ancient times as well.

So how should you enjoy Proverbs? Look for the major themes around which these diverse sayings cluster. How much is common sense? What kind of guidance for balance in your life do you find here? There will certainly be a wide variety of material. Don't try to find a single, coherent order to these sayings. There probably isn't any. But notice instruction on a variety of themes such as family, children, marriage, commitment to God, money, work, the use of the tongue, honesty, integrity, worship, and a good many others. You will also find humor in many of the proverbs. Reading them may even enhance your own sense of humor. Notice also how many seem just as true to life today as they did many centuries ago. Finally enjoy the wide range of advice, from the deeply spiritual to the humorous observations about everyday life, demonstrated by the two following proverbs:

"The fear of the Lord is the beginning of knowledge;
  fools despise wisdom and instruction" (Proverbs 1:7).

"'Bad, bad,' says the buyer,
  then goes away and boasts" (Proverbs 20:14).

Job

From reading Proverbs you could easily conclude that if you just do all the right things you will prosper and all will go well. As Proverbs 22:4 portrays life:

"The reward for humility and fear of the Lord
  is riches and honor and life."

The wisdom of Job questions this conventional wisdom and portrays a man who does everything right and still suffers miserably. Job is not an easy book to read, but it is well worth the effort. Here are few tips for enjoying this profound exploration of the problem of suffering.

Since Job is a long book, it will help to keep track of the flow of the outline. It begins and ends with a prose prologue and epilogue that gives the basic story of Job. Most of the book is poetry and falls between these two. The poetry consists of Job's complaints, his friends' attempts to "comfort" him, and finally God's response. It is sometimes hard to follow the dialogue and see who is speaking, and not everyone agrees on the divisions, but here is a basic outline that might help you keep track of the dialogue. (The numbers in parentheses are the chapters.)

Prologue (1-2)

Job (3)
Eliphaz (4-5)
Job (6-7)
Bildad (8)
Job (9-10)
Zophar (11)
Job (12-14)
Eliphaz (15)
Job (16-17)
Bildad (18)
Job (19)
Zophar (20)
Job (21)
Eliphaz (22)
Job (23-24)
Bildad (25)
Job (26-31; including a hymn to wisdom in 28)
Elihu (32-37)
God (38:1 - 40:2)
Job (40:3-5)
God (40:6 - 41:34)
Job (42:1-6)
Epilogue (42:7-17)

According to the basic story, Job is a devout, wealthy man who has everything, but Satan claims that he only serves God for what he gets. God gives Satan permission to take everything from Job, including his health. Job's friends come to dialogue with him and to convince him that what has happened is punishment for his sin. Job maintains his innocence. Finally, Job encounters God, and in the epilogue, a mirror image of the prologue, Job's fortunes are restored. In the course of this combination of prose story and poetic dialogue, Job offers various possibilities for the problem of evil and suffering.

The prologue speaks of Job's suffering as being Satan's work. The friends are convinced that Job's misfortunes come from his own sin. Job himself has a different explanation. Conventional wisdom speaks of the great patience of Job, but when you read these dialogues, Job complains bitterly, expresses strong laments such as we have seen in the Psalms, and blames God. According to Job, his suffering comes because, although he is innocent, God is against him. For example, in Job 19:7-11 he complains:

> "Even when I cry out, 'Violence!' I am not answered;
>   I call aloud, but there is no justice.
> He has walled up my way so that I cannot pass,
>   and he has set darkness upon my paths.
> He has stripped my glory from me,
>   and taken the crown from my head.
> He breaks me down on every side, and I am gone,
>   he has uprooted my hope like a tree.
> He has kindled his wrath against me,
>   and counts me as his adversary."

And in Job 16:11-17 he cries out:

> "God gives me up to the ungodly,
>   and casts me into the hands of the wicked.
> I was at ease, and he broke me in two;
>   he seized me by the neck and dashed me to pieces;

he set me up as his target;
   his archers surround me.
He slashes open my kidneys, and shows no mercy;
   he pours out my gall on the ground.
He bursts upon me again and again;
   he rushes at me like a warrior.
I have sewed sackcloth upon my skin,
   and have laid my strength in the dust.
My face is red with weeping,
   and deep darkness is on my eyelids,
though there is no violence in my hands,
   and my prayer is pure."

And there is yet another answer to the problem. God asks Job a series of questions that he cannot answer, such as where was Job when the world was made, implying that the answer may simply be above Job's pay grade. As you read this profound work, ask yourself which of these possibilities makes the most sense to you. One thing that the epilogue of the book makes very clear is that Job's friends had it all wrong. God tells them their only hope is for Job to pray for them. To what extent can you identify with Job? Does this book speak to real life questions that you struggle with?

The Five Little Scrolls

In the Hebrew Bible, five small books were called the five scrolls, or *megilloth,* and were grouped together. They are Song of Songs, Ecclesiastes, Lamentations, Esther, and Ruth. Some are stories and some are poetry. In later Jewish tradition all are associated with special days of either feasting or fasting.

Ruth is a delightful story, complete with suspense, plot twists, reversals, and a surprise ending. As you read, look for the many occurrences of the word *return*. What do you make of these? Notice also the use of the term *wing* in Ruth 2:12 and 3:9 (in some versions). Consider how many elements in this story are much like the conventions in the modern romantic comedy, where it seems like all is lost and then everything comes together in a surprising way. Look also for the prayers in Ruth. Are they all answered? If so, how are they answered? What does this suggest about prayer? In what way might this short and surprising story be transformative in your own life?

Esther is the only book in the Old Testament that is not found, at least in fragment, among the Dead Sea Scrolls. Maybe this is because it never mentions the name of God. It is the story of a brave young girl who, at considerable risk to herself, saves her people. The book gives the origins of the Jewish festival of Purim, which is celebrated to this day by Jews throughout the world around the month of March. Children wear costumes and the book of Esther is read to them. Notice in Esther the origin of the expression "For such a time as this."

Song of Songs, or Song of Solomon, is the book that brings giggles to kids when they discover it. It is a collection of love poetry that is quite sexually explicit in places. Through the centuries that has been sufficiently embarrassing to readers that they often allegorize it to make it about something else. This is unfortunate, for it detracts from the value of the poetry as an affirmation of the goodness of marital love and sexuality. Of course, while avoiding allegory, Christians cannot help but remember that in the New Testament human love is often used as a symbol for conveying God's love for us. That analogy only works when we grasp that sexuality is a gift of the Creator. Song of Songs is a vivid reminder of that truth.

Ecclesiastes is one of the strangest books in the Bible. Much of it seems quite pessimistic. The work begins with the thought that all is vanity or meaningless.

> "Vanity of vanities, says the Teacher,
>   vanity of vanities! All is vanity.
> What do people gain from all the toil
>   at which they toil under the sun?
> A generation goes, and a generation comes,
>   but the earth remains forever" (Ecclesiastes 1:2-4).

Ecclesiastes repeats this theme many times. Like the prophets, the author recoils at evil and injustice in the world.

> "Again I saw all the oppressions that are practiced under the sun. Look, the tears of the oppressed—with no one to comfort them! On the side of their oppressors there was power—with no one to comfort them. And I thought the dead, who have already died, more fortunate than the living, who are still alive; but better than both is the one who has not yet been, and has not seen the evil deeds that are done under the sun" (Ecclesiastes 4:1-3).

Ecclesiastes, like Job, is wisdom literature that is critical of the conventional wisdom literature of the day, as presented in a work like Proverbs. It reflects on the feeling of the absence of God. It is much more a series of reflections on life rather than a carefully constructed argument. And yet, throughout the reflections there are moments of positive optimism about life as well. See how these reflections resonate with your own feelings. Is the book too negative for you? Why do you think the Bible includes such honest reflections? Are there ways that they can be comforting?

Lamentations is exactly what the name implies, a series of laments over the destruction of Jerusalem by the Babylonians. As in some of the psalms of lament, this series of five laments (corresponding to the five chapters) doesn't end in cheerful resolution. It ends with a prayer for resolution that expresses something less than total confidence.

> "But you, O Lord, reign forever;
>   your throne endures to all generations.
> Why have you forgotten us completely?
>   Why have you forsaken us these many days?
> Restore us to yourself, O Lord, that we may be restored;
>   renew our days as of old—
> unless you have utterly rejected us,
>   and are angry with us beyond measure" (Lamentations 5:19-22).

These poems make use of literary devices not apparent in translation. Four of the five are acrostics. (See above on Psalm 119.) Much of the work uses a rhythm that was associated with mourning and dirges. The pattern has three emphasized beats in the first half of the line and two in the second (Da-Da-Da, Da-Da), which imitates the sound of mourning. Although most of the work expresses sorrow and mourning, there is some light in the middle of the tunnel, if not at the end. Chapter 3, verses 22-24, celebrates the faithfulness of God that is new every morning. These verses have served as the basis for some familiar Christian hymns. Most of the book, however, is quite mournful. Contemporary readers may tire of the laments found here and in the Psalms, but is it possible that our own worship experience could be enhanced by honest laments? I have attended some worship services where those who suffered the loss of a loved one in the previous year came together to both mourn and find comfort, and I have always found them very meaningful to the mourners. We might find greater comfort if we learned to lament.

Daniel

Daniel and Revelation are the two "apocalyptic" works in our Bible. This genre of literature uses an array of symbolic language to speak of the ultimate consummation of history and to understand the present in light of the final outcome. There were many such works that we do not consider a part of inspired Scripture. Yet neither of the apocalyptic works in our Bible fully fits this genre. As we have already seen, the book of Revelation also has the characteristics of a letter. Daniel, in addition to apocalyptic visions, begins with a series of stories about Daniel and his companions. Daniel was carried off to Babylon as a young man and lived to become an important figure in the foreign court.

No one will deny that parts of Daniel are difficult to interpret. But here are some tips. First pay attention to the stories. Notice how God leads and delivers in spite of seemingly impossible situations. You will find a lot of repetition in the telling of the stories. For example, in Daniel 3, the story of the fiery furnace, notice the repetition of the list of governmental officials and of the list of instruments. Part of this may well have been due to the oral telling of the story. Such repetition aids memory. It is inspiring to see the faithfulness of Daniel's companions who believed that even though they knew God could rescue them, they would be faithful even if God did not.

> "If our God whom we serve is able to deliver us from the furnace of blazing fire and out of your hand, O king, let him deliver us. But if not, be it known to you, O king, that we will not serve your gods and we will not worship the golden statue that you have set up" (Daniel 3:17-18).

After enjoying the stories, which, of course, include visions, move into the last half of the book with the message and situation of the stories in mind. Pay close attention to how many of the prophecies the book interprets for you. This makes it easier to follow. Can you deduce from these parts of the visions what is symbolized by other parts of the visions where the interpretation is not explicitly given? And even where you may not understand all the symbolism, is there a message about God and His will for humans that works its way through these visions? And don't think that the visions have only to do with historical facts. You will find spiritually inspiring material, such as the poignancy of Daniel's prayer in chapter 9. And don't be discouraged if you don't understand it all. The plethora of contrasting interpretations you will find in commentaries for Daniel 11 and 12, for example, proves that not everything is readily understandable. It will help a lot, however, if you familiarize yourself with the history of the kingdoms of Babylon, Medo-Persia, Greece, and Rome.

Ezra and Nehemiah

These two works from the "writings" section of the Old Testament are historical accounts of the Jews who returned to Israel after the Babylonian captivity, the time period of the prophets Haggai and Zechariah. They were originally one book in the Hebrew Bible. It covers snapshots of the history of the returned exiles over a period of almost a hundred years (536-444) as they attempted to rebuild the temple and the walls of Jerusalem. Notice the memoirs of Ezra and Nehemiah within this history, and pay attention to the struggles these former exiles have from within and without as they try to rebuild both physical structures and community.

One of the significant areas for contemplation is the relationship of God's people to the outside world. How much separation from the world should exist to assure faithfulness to God? The stance of Ezra/Nehemiah seems quite different from the spirit of Jonah. Where do you think Christians should stand today?

Some of the material in these books will be very inspiring, such as Ezra's prayer in Nehemiah 9. Some of it will be troubling. The methods used by Nehemiah to ensure faithfulness to God and separation from the other nations will seem extreme indeed, as the following passage demonstrates:

> "In those days also I saw Jews who had married women of Ashdod, Ammon, and Moab; and half of their children spoke the language of Ashdod, and they could not speak the language of Judah, but spoke the language of various peoples. And I contended with them and cursed them and beat some of them and pulled out their hair; and I made them take an oath in the name of God, saying, 'You shall not give your daughters to their sons, or take their daughters for your sons or for yourselves'" (Nehemiah 13:23-25).

It is amazing how strange these two books can seem, as they obviously come from another time and place. Yet it is equally amazing how relevant some of the basic questions they encounter are in our world and to our faith.

In a previous section we have already treated the books of 1 and 2 Chronicles, but we should note that they are a part of the "writings" section of the Hebrew Bible and should be included here.

For the Individual

1. Read Proverbs 20 and consider the following questions.

    a. Is there any theme that runs through these short, disparate sayings?

    b. How many areas of life do the proverbs in this chapter touch?

    c. How many of these proverbs do you find useful today? Are there any that you find so helpful you might memorize them and keep them in your mind for future use?

    d. What is your favorite proverb in this chapter? Why do you like it?

2. Read two psalms, Psalm 13 and Psalm 100.

    a. Compare and contrast these two psalms. How are they the same and how are they different?

    b. Look at the various types of psalms mentioned in Chapter Thirteen of the book and classify both of these psalms. What are the specific elements in each psalm that lead you consider it a specific type?

    c. What conventions of Hebrew poetry can you identify in each psalm?

    d. How and under what circumstances might you use each of these psalms in your prayer life?

For the Group

1. Compare and contrast your reactions to the sayings in Proverbs 20. Did you have the same favorites? Discuss the usefulness of these kinds of proverbs for your daily life.

2. Compare and contrast your reactions to Psalms 13 and 100. Did you agree on the classification of each?

    a. The mood of these two psalms is quite different. How often do you find yourself in the mood of each? How helpful to you personally are these psalms when you share such moods?

b. Try to prepare a worship experience for your group that would incorporate these two psalms; also include other elements such as hymns, prayers, testimonies, etc. Pick a time to gather and experience this worship service together.

3. As you come to the end of these guides, discuss what you have learned and how you might have grown from this experience. Would you like to see the group continue to meet with a different book and set of guides?

4. What are the most memorable ways you have encountered God through the entire experience of reading individually and sharing in the group? How will this study influence your future involvement in reading the Bible?

Epilogue

In some ways this book has been an audacious undertaking. Enjoying a *book* in the 21st century? Much of our culture seems to have moved beyond books to far more interactive forms of media.

Attending the birthday party of one my grandsons made this painfully clear. It was a time of great fun. The kids ran around outside soaking each other with squirt guns and hoses, frolicking with a puppy, and eating cake and ice cream. But the activity that captivated their attention the most was playing video games. The competition was fierce, the noise was deafening, and the huge screen was alive with booms, bangs, and explosions. I couldn't begin to keep up with all that was going on as they feverishly pushed all those buttons on their handheld remotes. At one point my grandson decided I had to give it a try. He tried to give me instructions, and after a little practice we played a game. He beat me by a score of 2,990 to 10!

In a world of such explosive excitement, can we still enjoy a book? I believe with all my heart that the answer is yes. I have seen God's power through the Holy Spirit use the Bible to transform lives. I think of one of my students. An alcoholic. Literally on the street. As he staggered down the street looking for a warm spot to land for a few minutes, he wandered into a hall where a preacher was sharing a message from the Bible. He listened, and the Spirit spoke to his heart. Today he is a pastor.

My hope and prayer is that this little book will not be something you simply read and then put away, but that it will be a catalyst to assist you in opening the Bible and reading it. Not only reading it, however, but enjoying it. Delighting in it. Finding the kind of the joy that the author of Psalm 119 found when he spoke of rejoicing in God's word, treasuring it, and delighting in it. And not only enjoying it, but finding new life in it—for ultimately the joy is not in the book itself, but in the gracious God to whom it points and who speaks through it.

The word *enjoying* in the title of this book doesn't refer to momentary happiness, but to the deep spiritual joy that Jesus talks about in the beatitudes of the Sermon on the Mount in Matthew 5. That is the profound spiritual enjoyment of finding a God who loves us, transforms us, and promises us eternal life.

When your heart has been touched by God's transforming power through the Bible, then and only then will this book have served its purpose. May God bless you as you continue to read, enjoy, understand, and above all find peace, joy, and hope in the God of grace who revealed Himself in Jesus, the divine and eternal Word, and continues to speak to us in the Bible through the Holy Spirit.